9-23

Pittsburgh Series in Bibliography

EMILY DICKINSON

Emily Dickinson

A DESCRIPTIVE BIBLIOGRAPHY

Joel Myerson

UNIVERSITY OF
PITTSBURGH PRESS
1984

Published by the University of Pittsburgh Press, Pittsburgh, Pa. 15260
Copyright © 1984, University of Pittsburgh Press
All rights reserved
Feffer and Simons, Inc., London
Manufactured in the United States of America

Library of Congress Cataloging in Publication Data

Myerson, Joel.
  Emily Dickinson : a descriptive bibliography.

  "Principal works about Dickinson": p. 155
  Includes indexes.
  1. Dickinson, Emily, 1830–1886—Bibliography.
I. Title.
Z8230.5.M96   1984   [PS1541]   016.811′4   83-21678
ISBN 0-8229-3491-4

for Gwenne Myerson

Contents

Acknowledgments

IN compiling this bibliography I have incurred many debts of gratitude. I wish to express my appreciation to the following institutions and their staffs for help in using their collections during my visits to them: Amherst College, Boston Athenæum, Boston Public Library, The British Library, Brown University (Harris Collection of American Poetry), Cambridge University, Columbia University, Duke University, Edinburgh University, Garrett Theological Seminary, Harvard University (Houghton and Widener libraries), Jones Library, Library of Congress, Little, Brown and Company, New York Public Library (Berg Collection), The Newberry Library, Northwestern University, Oxford University (Bodleian Library), Princeton University (Margaret Jane Pershing Collection), Stanford University, University of Florida (Parkman D. Howe Collection), University of North Carolina, University of South Carolina, University of Toronto, University of Virginia (Clifton Waller Barrett Library of American Literature), University of Wisconsin, and Yale University (Beinecke and Sterling libraries). Harriet Oglesby of the University of South Carolina library was especially helpful in obtaining books for me on loan.

Many people have helped me in this project and I would especially like to thank the following: William R. Cagle, Jane M. Carey, Virginia Creeden, Rosemary Cullen, Edward L. Doctoroff, R. W. Franklin, Tako Furukawa, Ann Gross, Robert A. Gross, Harrison M. Hayford, Jo Hayford, Sidney Ives, John Lancaster, Richard Layman, Erika C. D. Lindemann, Daniel Lombardo, Richard M. Ludwig, Charles W. Mann, George Monteiro, Deborah Reilly, Carmen Russell, Barton Levi St. Armand, Ernest Starr, Lola Szladits, G. Thomas Tanselle, Eleanor M. Tilton, Elizabeth Witherell, and Bobbi Zonghi. Richard Taylor has photographed the materials in my collection with his usual excellence. I am grateful to Jane Flanders for her skillful copyediting of this book.

The bibliographical groundwork for the study of many nineteenth-century American authors was laid by Jacob Blanck in his *Bibliography of American Literature*. Like other scholars, I have been greatly aided by this work.

An earlier version of this book was read by Willis J. Buckingham, Carlton Lowenberg, and William White, who all generously shared with me their knowledge of Dickinson and information about items in their personal collections.

Matthew J. Bruccoli has been generous with his assistance and this bibliography is much the better for it.

A fellowship from the John Simon Guggenheim Memorial Foundation greatly facilitated the research and preparation of this book. I wish to thank the Guggenheim Foundation for its support.

The University of South Carolina has provided material support for the preparation of this book. I am grateful to the Research and Productive Scholarship Committee, to Chester Bain, dean of the College of Humanities and Social Sciences, and to George L. Geckle, chairman of the department of English, for help. I also wish to thank my research assistant, Caroline Bokinsky, for her valuable assistance.

I am grateful to Amherst College and Yale University for permission to quote from manuscripts in their possession. I am equally grateful to the following libraries for permission to reproduce photographs of materials in their possession: Amherst College, Brown University, Princeton University, University of Virginia, and Yale University. The Roberts Brothers records are used with the permission of Little, Brown and Company. The frontispiece is reproduced by permission of the Trustees of Amherst College.

Greta has once again endured my bibliopoly and periodic disappearances. Her patience and love have helped make this book possible.

Introduction

THIS descriptive bibliography of the works of Emily Dickinson is limited to writings by Dickinson. Writings about Dickinson are not listed except in cases where they include something by Dickinson published for the first time.

FORMAT

Section A lists chronologically all books by Dickinson, including all printings of all editions through 1982.

The numbering system for Section A indicates the edition and printing for each entry. Thus, for *Poems: Third Series, A 4.1.a* indicates that this is the fourth title by Dickinson published (*A 4*), and that the entry describes the first edition (*1*), first printing (*a*). Issues are indicated by subscript numbers—thus *A 6.1.f₂* is the second issue of the sixth printing of *Further Poems*. States are discussed in the text.

Each entry begins with a facsimile of the title page (with its dimensions given) and, where relevant, the copyright page, then pagination information and a collation of the gatherings. Information on typography and paper includes the dimensions of the printed text, type of paper, number of lines per page, and running heads. Thus 5″ × 3″ indicates the height and width of the area containing the text on a page; 5″ (4½″) × 3″ indicates the height (first from the top of the running head to the bottom of the last line of text, and second from the top of the first line of text to the bottom of the last line of text) and width of the printed area. When relevant, information on sheet bulk is given. All paper is white unless otherwise indicated. Binding information includes cloth types, descriptions of stampings, and notes on flyleaves, endpapers, page trimming, and page-edge gilding or staining. Dust jackets, when present, are fully described and usually reproduced.[1] Information on publication is drawn from the diaries and letters of Dickinson's editors and publishers; publishers' records; copyright information (from both published and manuscript records of the Copyright Office); and contemporary book trade announcements. Locations are provided to identify the libraries holding copies of each title described. Notes give information not discussed elsewhere in the entry.

Section B lists chronologically all miscellaneous collections of Dickinson's writings in English through 1982. Included are bilingual collections. Bindings

---

1. Exceptions are unprinted glassine dust jackets.

are assumed to be cloth or boards unless otherwise indicated. Locations are given for the copies examined.

Section C lists chronologically all titles in which material by Dickinson appears for the first time in a book or pamphlet. Entries within a year are arranged alphabetically when publication information is not known. Included are poetry and letters.[2] All items are signed unless otherwise indicated. Previously published materials are so identified. The first printings only of these titles are described, but English editions and selected reprintings are also noted. Binding is assumed to be cloth or boards unless otherwise indicated. Locations are given for the copies examined.

Section D lists chronologically all first American and English publications in newspapers and magazines of material by Dickinson through 1982. All items are signed unless otherwise indicated.

Section E lists chronologically material falsely attributed to Dickinson.

An *appendix* lists principal works about Dickinson.

An *index to the poems* provides a printing history for each of Dickinson's poems.

TERMS AND METHODS

Edition. All copies of a book printed from a single setting of type—including all reprintings from standing type, from plates, or by photo-offset processes.

Printing. All copies of a book printed at one time (without moving the type or plates from the press).

State. States occur only within single printings and are created by an alteration not affecting the conditions of publication or sale to *some* copies of a given printing (by stop-press correction or cancellation of leaves). There must be two or more states.

Issue. Issues occur only within single printings and are created by an alteration affecting the conditions of publication or sale to *some* copies of a single printing (usually a title leaf alteration). There cannot be a first issue without a second.

Edition, printing, state, and *issue* have here been restricted to the sheets of the book.[3]

Dust jackets for Section A entries have been described in detail because they are part of the original publication effort and sometimes provide information about how the book was marketed. There is, of course, no certainty that a jacket now on a book was always on it.

For binding-cloth designations I have used the method proposed by G.

---

2. No attempt has been made to identify the many poems by Dickinson set to music; see, for examples, *Bibliography of American Literature* 2:448–51.

3. An argument could be made for extending the definition of *issue* in nineteenth-century books to include bindings as well. For example, the Roberts Brothers printings of Dickinson's poems were bound in Little, Brown and Company casings (with Roberts Brothers title pages) after June 1898, when Roberts Brothers was purchased by Little, Brown. In such cases it is difficult to avoid regarding the different bindings as *issues* because they do represent a deliberate attempt to alter the conditions of publication.

Thomas Tanselle;[4] most of these cloth grains are illustrated in Jacob Blanck, ed., *Bibliography of American Literature* (New Haven: Yale University Press, 1955–).

Color specifications are based on the *ISCC-NBS Color Name Charts Illustrated with Centroid Colors* (National Bureau of Standards). Centroid numbers have not been assigned; instead, the general color designations have been used.[5]

The spines of bindings or dust jackets are printed horizontally unless otherwise indicated. The reader is to assume that vertically printed spines read from top to bottom unless otherwise indicated.

Copyright on Dickinson's early works was registered with the Copyright Office in two stages: first, the book's title was given and entered into the copyright books, then a copy of the published work was deposited. Both these dates are given when available.

This bibliography also makes use of deposit and inscribed copies to help determine publication dates. Dates given for copies at BC, BE, BL, BO, and DLC are the dates written or stamped on the copies deposited for copyright or received at those institutions. Dates given for copies at other institutions indicate either the date the copy was received into the collection or a date inscribed by a contemporary owner of the book. In all cases, these dates list either the month and year, or the day, month, and year; a parenthetical year-only date after a location indicates the year of publication (usually as determined from title page or copyright information) of a later reprinting of a work at that institution.

Some of the collected editions of Dickinson's works were sold in series. When the series is identified in the work (such as on the title page or the binding), it is italicized. When the series is unidentified but can be ascertained from publishers' records or contemporary book trade announcements, it is placed within quotation marks.

The publication history of Dickinson's poems and letters is one that causes problems for the bibliographer.[6] Apparently Dickinson herself prepared nothing for publication; the few works by her published during her lifetime were most likely published without her consent or knowledge. All of her book-length works were published posthumously by editors who each had different editorial principles. Moreover, nearly all of Dickinson's manuscript poems are

---

4. G. Thomas Tanselle, "The Specifications of Binding Cloth," *The Library* 21 (September 1966), 246–47. The reader should also consult Tanselle's excellent "The Bibliographical Description of Patterns," *Studies in Bibliography* 23 (1970), 72–102, which reproduces all of the cloth grains illustrated in *Bibliography of American Literature* plus additional ones.

5. See G. Thomas Tanselle, "A System of Color Identification for Bibliographical Description," *Studies in Bibliography* 20 (1967), 203–34, for a discussion of how this system can be fully employed. I feel, however, that the use of exact Centroid color designations creates a false sense of precision, especially for nineteenth-century books. Oxidation, fading, wear, and nonuniform dyeing practices make precise color identification difficult, if not impossible. In any case, color identification by the Centroid system is inexact.

6. For the history of the editing and publication of Dickinson's poems, see Millicent Todd Bingham, *Ancestors' Brocades* (New York: Harper's, 1945), and R. W. Franklin, *The Editing of Emily Dickinson* (Madison: University of Wisconsin Press, 1967).

untitled, and most of those published with titles had their titles made up and supplied by her editors. To deal with this situation, I refer to Dickinson's poems in two ways: if the poem is untitled, I give the first line; if the poem is titled, I give the title, followed by the first line in brackets. In both cases, capitalization and spelling are given as they appear in the text being referred to, rather than to the text as established by Thomas H. Johnson in 1955 (see A 10). However, for easy reference each poem is identified by its number in Johnson's edition.[7] Thus, *P 123* refers to poem number 123 in *The Poems of Emily Dickinson* (A 10). An *index to the poems* provides at a glance the printing history of each poem, starting with its first appearance in print. The *index to the poems* is arranged alphabetically by the first line in each poem (as it appears in Johnson's edition); titled poems are listed in the general index to this book.

A different problem arises with Dickinson's letters: most of them are un-dated. When dates and the names of recipients are not given in the book or article being referred to, I have supplied them in brackets according to the information supplied in Johnson's 1958 edition of the letters (see A 11). For easy reference, each letter is identified by its number in Johnson's edition. Thus *L 123* refers to letter number 123 in *The Letters of Emily Dickinson* (A 11).

Because Dickinson is a highly collectable author, I have been more gener-ous than usual in describing the later reprintings of the three volumes of her poetry published by Roberts Brothers and Little, Brown. In those instances where changes in pagination, collation, signing, contents, and/or paper type distinguish a new printing, such information is given for that entry. Unless new information is given, the reader should assume that these items are the same for that entry as they were in the preceding printing. Information is also given about the bindings noted for later printings.

This bibliography is based upon evidence gathered from my personal in-spection and collation of multiple copies of Dickinson's works. For first En-glish and American editions, only libraries holding copies that are biblio-graphically intact (not rebound or repaired) are listed. Exceptions are re-bound copies containing nonbibliographical information, such as dated owners' inscriptions, which is mentioned in notes. The symbols used for American libraries are those employed by the *National Union Catalog;* those for Canadian libraries are the same as those listed in *Symbols of Canadian Libraries,* 7th ed. (Ottawa: National Library of Canada, 1977), which are here preceded by *Ca;* those for British libraries are the same as those listed in the *British Union-Catalogue of Periodicals,* which are here preceded by *B.* The following are additional symbols:

Buckingham	Collection of Willis J. Buckingham
JM	Collection of Joel Myerson
Lowenberg	Collection of Carlton Lowenberg
White	Collection of William White

---

7. Readers should be aware that the new edition of Dickinson's poems being prepared by R. W. Franklin will supersede Johnson's texts, as well as renumber the poems.

This bibliography is not an attempt to indicate the scarcity of Dickinson's works and should not be taken as such. If there is only one location listed, it means that, of all the libraries I visited and corresponded with, only one had or reported having a copy with all the examined points intact; it does not mean that there is only one copy of that work in existence.

A bibliography is outdated the moment it goes to the printer. Addenda and corrigenda are earnestly solicited.

Edisto Beach, South Carolina
17 July 1982

A. Separate Publications

All books by Dickinson, including all printings of all editions through 1982, arranged chronologically.

A 1 POEMS

A 1.1.a
First American edition, first printing (1890)

POEMS

BY

EMILY DICKINSON

Edited by two of her Friends

MABEL LOOMIS TODD AND T. W. HIGGINSON

BOSTON
ROBERTS BROTHERS
1890

A 1.1.a: 7″ × 4¾″

Copyright, 1890,

BY ROBERTS BROTHERS.

University Press:

JOHN WILSON AND SON, CAMBRIDGE.

[i–iii] iv–vi [vii] viii–xii [xiii–xvi] [13] 14–40 [41–42] 43–65 [66–68] 69–106 [107–108] 109–152

[1–19⁴ 20²] Signed [1]¹⁰ 2–9⁸ 10⁴

Contents: p. i: title page; p. ii: copyright page; pp. iii–vi: 'PREFACE.', signed 'THOMAS WENTWORTH HIGGINSON.'; pp. vii–xii: contents; p. xiii: eight lines of verse, beginning *'THIS is my letter to the world,'*; p. xiv: blank; p. xv: 'I. | LIFE.'; p. xvi: blank; pp. 13–40: poems; p. 41: 'II. | LOVE.'; p. 42: blank; pp. 43–65: poems; p. 66: blank; p. 67: 'III. | NATURE.'; p. 68: blank; pp. 69–106: poems; p. 107: 'IV | TIME AND ETERNITY.'; p. 108: blank; pp. 109–152: poems.

Typography and paper: 4³⁄₁₆″ (3⅞″) × 3″; calendered paper; sheets bulk ¹¹⁄₁₆″; preface: 22 lines per page; various lines per page for poetry. Running heads: rectos: p. v: *'PREFACE.'*; pp. ix–xi: *'CONTENTS.'*; pp. 15–39, 43–65, 69–105, 109–151: *'POEMS.'*; versos: pp. iv–vi: *'PREFACE.'*; pp. viii–xii: *'CONTENTS.'*; pp. 14–40, 44–64, 70–106, 110–152: *'POEMS.'*.

Binding: Two styles have been noted:

Binding A: Three-piece binding: medium gray V cloth (smooth) spine, extending over to meet white V cloth (smooth) on front and back covers, the meeting of the two cloths marked by a silverstamped wavy vertical rule; front cover: silverstamped '[ornate capitals] · POEMS · | [design] | [ornate printing] · Emily · Dickinson · | [Indian pipes]'; back cover: blank; spine: goldstamped '[ornate capitals] POEMS | [two lines in ornate printing] Emily | Dickinson | BOSTON | ROBERTS BROS.'. Quadruple calendered front flyleaves and double calendered back flyleaves; or coated front and back flyleaves; or no flyleaves. Wove, laid, or coated endpapers. Top edges trimmed, front and bottom edges rough-trimmed; or all edges trimmed. Top edges gilded.

Binding B: The same as Binding A, except: the first three lines on the front cover and wavy vertical rule on the front and back covers are goldstamped. Wove front flyleaf; or wove back flyleaf; or calendered back flyleaf; or no flyleaves. Wove or coated endpapers. Top edges trimmed, front and bottom edges rough-trimmed; or top and bottom edges trimmed, front edges rough-trimmed; or all edges trimmed. Top edges gilded.

Dust jacket: Unprinted light yellow-brown paper.

Box: Two-part (top and bottom) cardboard box covered with white glossy calendered paper, except on the insides of both parts and on the bottom of the bottom part. Unprinted.

Publication: 500 copies printed 8 October 1890. Price, $1.50.

Thomas Niles of Roberts Brothers wrote Higginson on 10 June 1890 that if Lavinia Dickinson "will pay for the plates, we will publish from them at our expense a small Ed, say 500, which shall be exempt from copyright [royalty], all future issues to be subject

Binding B for A 1.1.a

to 15% copyright on the retail price of all sold" (MA). This arrangement was modified in Lavinia's favor when it became obvious that sales were exceptional, and on 16 January 1891 Niles wrote Mrs. Todd, "We are quite willing to modify the original agreement by paying for the plates and copyright on all sold at ten per cent" (MA).

Higginson wrote Mrs. Todd on 14 July 1890 that he had "sent the MS. to Niles" that day (MA). On 30 July 1890 Niles wrote Mrs. Todd that Higginson had read "about 75 pages of proof" (CtY). Mrs. Todd received the "first proof" on 30 July 1890, returned the "final galley proofs" on 30 August 1890, and returned the "final set of plate proofs" on 25 September 1890 (*Ancestors' Brocades,* pp. 61, 66–67). On 4 October 1890 Niles wrote Mrs. Todd, "The book is printing" (MA). Niles sent "sheets" for review to William Dean Howells and Richard Henry Stoddard on 8 October 1890 (MA). On 20

October 1890 Mrs. Todd wrote in her diary, "A folded but unbound copy of the *Poems* came" (CtY; see *note five*). On 7 November 1890 six copies of the bound volume were sent to Mrs. Todd, and the next day she wrote in her diary, "Emily's volume came— complete, binding, design, all" (Niles to Mrs. Todd, MA; CtY). And on 12 November 1890 Mrs. Todd wrote in her diary, "Emily's volume published today" (CtY).

Advertised as "drab and white cloth with gilt design, gilt top," at $1.25, for 12 November 1890, in *Publishers' Weekly* 38 (8 November 1890), 686. Listed as "grey and white, with ornamental design in silver," at $1.25, in *Publishers' Weekly* 38 (8 November 1890), 667; at $1.50, in *Publishers' Weekly* 38 (15 November 1890), 695, 700. Deposited for copyright: title, 6 October 1890; book, 29 October 1890. Copyright registration A30843. Copyright renewed 26 January 1918. According to the publisher's records, published 12 November 1890. Deposit copies: Binding A: DLC (29 October 1890), two copies. Inscribed copies: Binding B: CtY (from Mrs. Todd, November 1890), MA (from Mrs. Todd, November 1890), MH (from Mrs. Todd, November 1890), ViU (from Mrs. Todd, November 1890), MA (from Mrs. Todd, 11 November 1890), NjP (25 December 1890). MBAt copy (rebound) received 18 November 1890. Royalty, 10% on all copies sold. Listed in the *English Catalogue* as an importation for December 1890 at 7s. 6d.

Printing: Electrotyped by John Wilson and Son. For printer's imprint, see copyright page illustration.

Locations: Binding A: DLC, RPB; Binding B: CtY (dust jacket, box), DLC, FU, ICN, IEN, InU, MA (two copies) (box), MAJ, MH, NN, NNC, NcU, NjP, PSt, RPB, ViU, WU.

Note one: A white silk ribbon marker is present in some copies.

Note two: Roberts Brothers, fearing that *Poems* would not sell well, chose to use calendered paper in order to bulk out the volume and thus make it appear thicker and a better buy for the money (see *Ancestors' Brocades*, p. 69n).

Note three: According to Mrs. Bingham, "The dainty binding, devised partly . . . in the hope of beguiling Christmas shoppers into buying the book for the beauty of its cover, was protected not only by a plain jacket but also by a shiny white pasteboard box made to fit" *(Ancestors' Brocades*, p. 69n).

Note four: For information on why the floral Indian pipes were chosen for the front cover and spine of *Poems*, see *Ancestors' Brocades*, p. 64; Mrs. Todd's original painting of the Indian pipes is reproduced in Sewall, *The Life of Emily Dickinson*, vol. 1, facing p. 179.

Note five: An unbound and unsewn set of folded and gathered signatures (measuring 7⅛″ × 4¾″, with all edges rough-trimmed and no gilding) has been noted: CtY.

Note six: Mrs. Todd and Higginson received $100 each for their work on *Poems* (*Ancestors' Brocades*, p. 109).

Note seven: On 11 December 1890 Niles wrote Mrs. Todd, "The book is out of print for the moment" (MA).

A 1.1.b
Second printing (1890)

Two issues have been noted:

A 1.1.b₁
First issue

Boston: Roberts Brothers, 1890.

Typography and paper: The same as in A 1.1.a, except: sheets bulk ⁹⁄₁₆″.

Binding: Two styles have been noted, priority undetermined:

> *Binding A:*   Three-piece binding: white V cloth (smooth) spine, extending over to meet medium gray V cloth (smooth) on front and back covers, the meeting of the two cloths marked by a silverstamped vertical straight rule; front cover: silverstamped the same as in A 1.1.a, Binding A; back cover: blank; spine: goldstamped the same as in A 1.1.a, Binding A. Coated flyleaves. Coated endpapers. Top and front edges trimmed, bottom edges rough-trimmed; or all edges trimmed. Top edges gilded.

> *Binding B:*   The same as Binding A, except: the meeting of the two cloths is marked by a goldstamped wavy vertical rule; coated back flyleaf; wove endpapers.

Publication: 380 copies printed 11 December 1890. According to the *Critic, Poems* had "passed to a second edition" (14 [6 December 1890], 297). Niles wrote Mrs. Todd on 11 December 1890 that he hoped to get the "2^d Ed. [out] in a day or two" (MA). On 16 December 1890, Mrs. Todd wrote in her diary, "Second edition of Emily's *Poems* out" (CtY). Inscribed copy: Binding A: MA (25 December 1890).

Locations: Binding A: MA, MH, White; Binding B: MB.

Note one: A red silk ribbon marker is present in some copies.

Note two: On 23 December 1890, Niles wrote Austin Dickinson, "I had to print a hurried second Ed. on a balance of paper wh. we had on hand. It amounted to only 400 copies." He also said that the "second edition" was "exhausted," a fact which Mrs. Todd wrote in her diary on the same date (*Ancestors' Brocades*, pp. 88–89; CtY).

A 1.1.b$_2$
Second issue

Boston: Roberts Brothers, 1891. The copyright page reads 'SECOND EDITION.'.

Collation: [1–19^4 $_{(\pm1_1)}$ 20^2]. Signed [1]^{10} 2–9^8 10^4. Three-piece binding of white shelf-back and medium gray covers—both V cloth (smooth).

Locations: JM, MB, MH.

Note: The cancel title leaf is inserted so carefully that it appears to be integral with leaf 1$_4$. However, the cancel title leaf is 6⅞″ high, whereas leaf 1$_4$ is 6¹⁵⁄₁₆″ high.

A 1.1.c
Third printing (1891)

Boston: Roberts Brothers, 1891.

'SECOND EDITION.'. Three-piece binding of white shelfback and medium gray covers—both V cloth (smooth). A red or white silk ribbon marker is present in some copies. Inscribed copies: InU (25 December 1890), MAJ (25 December 1890), NjP (25 December 1890), NjP (22 February 1891). *Locations:* InU, MAJ, NjP (two copies), RPB.

Note: The title leaf from this printing, which measures 6⅞″ high, is the one used as the cancel title leaf in A 1.1.b$_2$.

A 1.1.d
Fourth printing (1891)

Boston: Roberts Brothers, 1891. The copyright page reads 'THIRD EDITION.'.

Three states have been noted:

1st state: Gathering 2 is misfolded so that leaves 2_3 and 2_4 (containing, respectively, the poem "This is my letter to the world" and the half title to the first section) appear in the middle of the table of contents; see *note two*.

2nd state: Collation: $[1-19^4 \ _{-2_{1,2},+3_{1,2}} \ 20^2]$. See *note two* for an explanation of the cancelled and inserted leaves.

3rd state: Gathering 2 is folded correctly, so that leaves 2_3 and 2_4 are in the correct position; see *note two*.

Binding: All three states in a three-piece binding of white shelfback with medium gray covers—both V cloth (smooth).

Publication: 500 copies printed 23 December 1890. Niles wrote Mrs. Todd on 23 December 1890 that the "third edition" would "go to the binder to day. . . . For the third Ed., 500 copies, we were obliged to wait for the paper to be made" (MA). On 29 December 1890, Niles wrote Mrs. Todd that he was sending copies of the "third edition," "just in from the binder" (MA). According to Mrs. Bingham, published 27 December 1890 (*Ancestors' Brocades*, p. 109). Inscribed copy: 3d state: MAJ (1 January 1891). The *Critic* of 27 December 1890 noted that *Poems* had "passed to a third edition" (14, 340).

Locations: 1st state: MA, White; 2d state: CtY, NjP; 3d state: MAJ, WU.

Note one: A white silk ribbon marker is present in some copies.

Note two: On 3 January 1891, Niles wrote Mrs. Todd that all 250 copies of the "third edition" had been "bound up wrongly, a mistake of the folder in folding the title signature," and that 180 copies had been sold before the error was noticed (MA). And Mrs. Todd noted at the end of her diary for 1890 that she had bought four copies of the "third edition," but they were "returned, imperfectly bound" (CtY). Both are referring to an error in folding that resulted in gathering 2 being misfolded so that leaves 3 and 4 appear in the middle of the table of contents. These leaves were cancelled—the stubs remaining—and then pasted to the first leaf of gathering 3, where they took their proper place in the pagination sequence. Niles's statement that there were 250 copies in this printing must be in error; the publisher's records show that 500 copies were printed. He probably meant that 250 copies contained this error in folding, so that the number of copies of the first state may be as low as 70 (the copies unsold before the error was noticed) or as high as 70 plus the number of copies returned or recalled for cancelling and inserting the problem leaves.

Note three: On 16 January 1891, Niles wrote Mrs. Todd that 1,380 copies of the first three "editions" had been printed, with about 100 copies distributed gratis and the rest sold (MA).

A 1.1.e
Fifth printing (1891)

Boston: Roberts Brothers, 1891. The copyright page reads 'FOURTH EDITION.'.

Typography and paper: The same as in A 1.1.a, except: laid paper with horizontal chain marks $1^5/_{16}''$ apart.

Binding: Medium gray, dark green, or medium olive V cloth (smooth); bevelled edges; front cover: goldstamped '[ornate capitals] · POEMS · | [design] | [ornate printing] · Emily · Dickinson · | [Indian pipes]'; back cover: blank; spine: goldstamped the same as in A 1.1.a, Binding A. Laid flyleaves. Laid endpapers. Top edges trimmed, front and bottom edges rough-trimmed; or all edges trimmed. Top edges gilded.

Publication: 500 copies printed 24 January 1891. Price, $1.25. Niles wrote Mrs. Todd on 16 January 1891 that the "fourth edition" was "now printing," and the next day Mrs. Todd wrote in her diary, "Poems going at once into fourth edition" (MA; CtY). Niles sent copies of the "fourth edition" to Mrs. Todd on 29 January 1891, and the next day she wrote in her diary that she had received the copies, calling them "very prettily bound" (MA; CtY). Announced as a "new edition" with the price "reduced to $1.25, and the drab-and-white edition . . . discontinued," in *Publishers' Weekly* 39 (31 January 1891), 223. Announced as having "left the press," in *Book-Buyer* 8 (February 1891), 10 (Arlo Bates, "Literary Topics in Boston"). Inscribed copies: NjP (February 1891), MAJ (17 February 1891), MAJ (22 May 1891). Listed in the publisher's costbooks as the "cheap edition," probably because of the new price.

Locations: CtY, JM, MA, MAJ (two copies), NjP, RPB.

Note one: A red or white silk ribbon marker is present in some copies.

Note two: Niles wrote Mrs. Todd on 29 January 1891 of the new binding, "We do not intend to put them into boxes" (MA). According to Mrs. Bingham, "Since the 'instant and hearty recognition' seemed to assure the book a permanent place in libraries, a cover more desirable than the Christmas gift-book variety of the first and second editions was needed. So a cover of uniform color was substituted" (*Ancestors' Brocades,* pp. 80–81*n*).

Note three: On 12 February 1891 Mrs. Todd wrote in her diary that the "fourth edition" of *Poems* was "gone" (CtY).

Note four: The following textual variants between the fourth and fifth printings are present:

vi.7	conflict [struggle
20.11	cautions [cautious
29.1	afar [ajar
53.13–14	nothing, | Only, your [nothing, only | Your
54.9	sea, take me! [sea, | Take me!

Note five: The changes at 20.11, 53.13–14, and 54.9 were made at the suggestion of Mrs. Todd (see her letter to Higginson, 29 December 1890), and the change at 29.1 at the suggestion of Sue Dickinson (see her letter to Higginson, 4 January 1891, and Higginson's letter to Mrs. Todd, 5 January 1891) (*Ancestors' Brocades,* pp. 90–91, 92).

A 1.1.f
Sixth printing (1891)

Boston: Roberts Brothers, 1891. The copyright page reads 'FIFTH EDITION.'.

Binding: Medium gray or dark green V cloth (smooth) with bevelled edges.

Publication: 500 copies printed 8 February 1891. Mrs. Todd wrote in her diary on 12 February 1891 that the "fifth edition" was "in press" (CtY). On 17 February 1891, Niles wrote Mrs. Todd that the "5th [edition]" was "binding" (MA). Inscribed copy: Binding B: NN (22 April 1891).

Locations: CtY, MA, MAJ, MB, NN, NjP, WU.

Note one: A white silk ribbon marker is present in some copies.

Note two: On 11 March 1891, Niles wrote Mrs. Todd that the "fifth edition" was "selling well," with 250 copies remaining (MA).

A 1.1.g
Seventh printing (1891)

Two issues have been noted:

A 1.1.g$_1$
First issue

Boston: Roberts Brothers, 1891.

'SIXTH EDITION.'. Three-piece (medium yellow-green shelfback with white covers) binding, or medium gray or medium olive (with bevelled edges) casings—all V cloth (smooth). A red or white silk ribbon marker is present in some copies. 500 copies printed 14 March 1891. Niles wrote Mrs. Todd on 11 March 1891 that the "sixth edition" was "printing," and on 17 April 1891 Mrs. Todd wrote in her diary that she took two copies to Lavinia Dickinson (MA; CtY). Inscribed copies: MAJ (9 July 1891), NNC (2 August 1891), JM (25 December 1891). *Locations:* JM, MAJ, MH, NN, NNC, NjP.

Note: Copies of *Poems* in the three-piece bindings have had the page edges trimmed more than have those copies in single casings; the page size is usually ⅛″ smaller.

A 1.1.g$_2$
Second issue

Boston: Roberts Brothers, 1892.

'SEVENTH EDITION.'. Collation: $[1–19^4$ $_{+1_1, +1_2})$ $20^2]$; the title leaf has been cancelled and a cancel blank leaf pasted to the stub; a new title leaf is tipped on the front of leaf 1_2 (see *note*). Signed $[1]^{11}$ $2–9^8$ 10^2. Medium gray V cloth (smooth) with bevelled edges. A white silk ribbon marker is present. *Location:* RPB.

Note: The copyright page of A 1.1.g$_2$ has 'U.S.A.' in the printer's imprint, indicating that it is from the eighth printing (see A 1.1.h, *note one*).

A 1.1.h
Eighth printing (1892)

Boston: Roberts Brothers, 1892.

'SEVENTH EDITION.'. Three-piece (medium yellow-green shelfback with white covers) binding, or medium gray or medium olive (with bevelled edges) casings—all V cloth (smooth). A white silk ribbon marker is present in some copies. 500 copies printed 11 July 1891. Mrs. Todd wrote in her diary on 16 June 1891 that the "seventh edition" was "either preparing or already out this week" (CtY). Inscribed copies: MA (1 August 1891), MAJ (25 December 1891), NjP (25 December 1891). *Locations:* CtY, JM, MA, MAJ, MH, NjP, RPB, WU.

Note one: The following variant between the seventh and eighth printings is present:

    ii.5   Cambridge. [Cambridge, U.S.A.

Note two: Copies have been noted with mixed sheets (both laid and calendered paper) from the eighth and one of the first four printings, in three-quarter white leather bindings, one with a moiré paper-covered cardboard box (see A 1.1.j, Binding C and *note two* for complete descriptions): CtY (box), MA. These may be from the "five extra copies, white, received Nov. 14," or from the "two leather-bound copies . . . to Vinnie [Lavinia Dickinson]" that Mrs. Todd refers to at the end of her diary for 1892 (CtY).

A 1.1.i
Ninth printing (1892)

Boston: Roberts Brothers, 1892. The copyright page reads 'EIGHTH EDITION.'.

Three states have been noted, priority undetermined:

1st state: Pagination, collation, signing, and contents are the same as in A 1.1.a.

2d state: A single-leaf gathering is before the title leaf (p. a: blank; p. b: advertisement for *Poems* and *Poems: Second Series*); pagination, collation, signing, and contents are affected accordingly.

3d state: A two-leaf gathering is before the title leaf (pp. a–c: blank; p. d: advertisement for *Poems* and *Poems: Second Series*); pagination, collation, signing, and contents are affected accordingly.

Binding: Three-piece (medium yellow-green shelfback with white covers) binding, or medium gray or medium olive (with bevelled edges) casings—all V cloth (smooth). A white silk ribbon marker is present in some copies.

Publication: 500 copies printed 2 October 1891. The *Nation* of 16 July 1891 noted that "the eighth American edition" of *Poems* was "already in preparation" (53, 48). Inscribed copy: 3rd state: JM (13 November 1891).

Locations: 1st state: NjP; 2d state: MBAt, NjP, RPB; 3d state: JM, MA, NjP.

A 1.1.j
Tenth printing (1892)

Boston: Roberts Brothers, 1892. The copyright page reads 'NINTH EDITION.'.

Two states have been noted, priority undetermined:

1st state: Collation: $[1^1 \ 2-10^8 \ 11^6]$. Signed $[1]^{11} \ 2-9^8 \ 10^4$. A single-leaf gathering is before the title leaf (p. a: blank; p. b: advertisement for *Poems* and *Poems: Second Series*); pagination and contents are affected accordingly.

2d state: Collation: $[1^2 \ 2-10^8 \ 11^6]$. Signed $[1]^{12} \ 2-9^8 \ 10^4$. A two-leaf gathering is before the title leaf (pp. a–c: blank; p. d: advertisement for *Poems* and *Poems: Second Series*); pagination and contents are affected accordingly.

Binding: Three styles have been noted, priority undetermined:

Binding A: Three-piece binding of medium yellow-green shelfback with white covers—both V cloth (smooth).

Binding B: Medium gray or medium olive V cloth (smooth) with bevelled edges.

Binding C: Three-piece three-quarter white leather binding: white leather spine extending over to meet paper-covered boards of black floral patterns on a dark orange-yellow background, the meeting of the two marked by a goldstamped vertical straight rule; front and back covers: white leather outside corners with goldstamped rules where they meet the paper-covered boards; spine: six blindstamped boxes set off with goldstamped rules: boxes 1, 3, 5, and 6 with a goldstamped floral design, box 2 with a reddish brown morocco label with goldstamped '[within a single-rule frame] POEMS', and box 4 with a dark reddish brown morocco label with goldstamped '[all within a single-rule frame] EMILY | DICKINSON | * '. Back laid flyleaf. Endpapers of the same design as the paper covered boards. All edges trimmed. All edges gilded. See *note two*.

Box: Two-part (slipcase with covering for open end) cardboard box covered with white moiré paper; the slipcase part is fleece-lined. Unprinted. See *note two.*

Publication: 1,000 copies printed 9 November 1891. Inscribed copies: 2d state, Binding B: MA, NjP, WU (all 25 December 1891). Prices: Binding A, $1.50; Binding B: $1.25; Binding C: $3.50.

Locations: 1st state: Binding A: MA; Binding B: NjP; Binding C: MAJ, NjP, WU; 2d state: Binding A: JM, NjP; Binding B: CtY, JM, MA, MB, NjP, WU.

Note one: A white silk ribbon marker is present in some copies.

Note two: Mrs. Bingham reports, from the "publishers' announcement": "Bound in Pure White Calf Backs and Corners, with dainty Paper Sides, gold edges, lettering and finish in gold, enclosed in fleece-lined boxes" (*Ancestors' Brocades,* p. 412; copy, MA). Like the other three-piece bindings, the sheets of the three-quarter leather copies are trimmed about ⅛″ smaller than are those of the single casings (see *note* to A 1.1.g). On 9 November 1891, E. D. Hardy of Roberts Brothers wrote David Todd and enclosed two copies of "½ white calf of the 1st Series" (MA).

A 1.1.k

Boston: Roberts Brothers, 1892.

'TENTH EDITION.'. Pagination, collation, signing, and contents are the same as in A 1.1.j, 2d state. Three-piece (medium yellow-green shelfback with white covers) binding, or medium gray or medium olive (with bevelled edges) casings—all V cloth (smooth). A white silk ribbon marker is present in some copies. 1,000 copies printed 24 December 1891. Inscribed copies: WU (14 February 1892), MAJ (14 May 1892), WU (July 1892). *Locations:* CtY, JM, MA, MAJ, NN, NcU, NjP, OCIW, PBm, RPB, WU (two copies).

A 1.1.l

Boston: Roberts Brothers, 1892.

'ELEVENTH EDITION.'. Three-piece (medium yellow-green shelfback with white covers) binding, or medium gray (with bevelled edges) casing—all of V cloth (smooth). A white silk ribbon marker is present in some copies. 500 copies printed 3 September 1892. *Locations:* IEN, MA, MAJ, NNC, NjP, ViU.

A 1.1.m

Boston: Roberts Brothers, 1893.

'ELEVENTH EDITION.'. Medium gray or medium olive (with bevelled edges) V cloth (smooth) casings, or three-piece three-quarter white leather binding. A white silk ribbon marker is present in some copies. 280 copies printed 14 March 1893. *Locations:* IEN, JM, MA, NNC, NjP, WU.

A 1.1.n

Boston: Roberts Brothers, 1893. The copyright page reads 'ELEVENTH EDITION.'. Bound with *Poems: Second Series,* 'SIXTH EDITION' (A 2.1.g), in two-volumes-in-one format.

[a–d]; pp. i–152 are the same as in A 1.1.a; [i–vi]; pp. 1–232 are the same as in A 2.1.a.

[1² 2–10⁸ 11⁶ a¹ 1⁸] 2–12⁸ [13]⁸ 14⁸ 15⁴   Signed [1]¹² 2–9⁸ 10⁴ [1]⁹ 2–12⁸ [13]⁸ 14⁸ 15⁴. A two-leaf gathering on calendered paper with a manuscript facsimile is inserted after leaf a₁.

Contents: pp. a–c: blank; p. d: advertisement for *Poems* and *Poems: Second Series;* pp. 1–152: the same as in A 1.1.a; p. i: half title for *Poems: Second Series;* p. ii: blank; pp. iii–iv: manuscript facsimile; pp. 1–232: the same as in A 2.1.a.

Typography and paper: Calendered paper.

Binding: Two styles have been noted, priority undetermined:

Binding A: Three-piece bindings of medium gray or light yellow-green shelfbacks with white covers—all V cloth (smooth).

Binding B: Full dark green leather: front and back covers: goldstamped crosses in each corner and goldstamped 2″ oval design in the center; spine: goldstamped '[three lines within a single-rule frame] POEMS | [rule] | DICKINSON | [within a single-rule frame] 1893'. Reddish brown wove endpapers with a gold floral pattern. Edges of inside front and back covers have gold tooling. All edges trimmed. All edges gilded. See *note two.*

Box: Two-part (top and bottom) cardboard box covered with white calendered paper, except on the insides of both parts and on the bottom of the bottom part. Written on the outside bottom of the bottom part is 'Dickinsons Poems | Ren No 10 | Green'. Printed in blue on the side of the top part is 'Dickinsons Poems RenNo10'. Used with Binding B only; see *note two.*

Publication: Inscribed copy: Binding A: MAJ (25 December 1893). Prices: Binding A, $2.00; Binding B, $4.00.

Locations: Binding A: JM, MA, MAJ; Binding B: CtY.

Note one: A white silk ribbon marker is present in some copies.

Note two: Mrs. Bingham, quoting from "Messrs. Roberts Brothers' Holiday Publications, 1893," notes copies "bound [two-volumes-in-one] in full crushed Turkey morocco of dainty colors, and decorated in a style which fully justifies the characteristic term 'Renaissance,' being a revival of the old English bindings in vogue some seventy or eighty years ago, which were adapted from various artistic designs used in the Middle Ages. The books are hand-finished in a chaste and beautiful manner, solid gold edges, rolled on the inside and outer edges of the covers" (*Ancestors' Brocades*, p. 414; copy, MA).

A 1.1.o

Boston: Roberts Brothers, 1893. The copyright page reads 'THIRTEENTH EDITION.'. Combined with *Poems: Second Series,* 'SEVENTH EDITION' (see A 2.1.h).

pp. i–152 are the same as in A 1.1.a; [i–vi]; pp. 1–230 are the same as in A 2.1.a.

[1–24⁸ 25²] Signed [1]¹⁰ 2–3⁸ [4]⁸ 5–9⁸ 10⁴ [1]⁹ 2–9⁸ [10]⁸ 11–12⁸ [13]⁸ 14⁸ 15⁴. A two-leaf gathering on calendered paper with a manuscript facsimile is inserted after leaf 10₇.

Contents: pp. 1–152 are the same as in A 1.1.a; p. i: 'POEMS | BY | EMILY | DICKINSON | [rule] | SECOND SERIES'; p. ii: blank; pp. iii–vi: facsimile of the manuscript of "Renunciation"; pp. 1–230 are the same as in A 2.1.a.

Typography and paper: Calendered paper.

Binding: Three-piece bindings of medium gray or medium yellow-green shelfbacks with white covers—all V cloth (smooth).

Publication: According to Mrs. Bingham, 500 copies printed; published May 1893 (*Ancestors' Brocades,* p. 414). According to the publisher's costbooks, 350 copies bound April 1893. Price, $2.00. Royalty, 25¢.

Locations: MA, MAJ, NjP, PSt, RPB, WU.

Note one: A white silk ribbon marker is present in some copies.

Note two: In some copies, the signature marks for gatherings 6 and 7 do not print: RPB, WU.

Note three: Gathering 10, which would normally end with the last page of text in *Poems,* now ends with leaves 7 and 8 containing, respectively, the half title and title leaves for *Poems: Second Series.*

A 1.1.p

Boston: Roberts Brothers, 1894.

'THIRTEENTH EDITION.'. Collation: $[1^2 \ 2-10^8 \ 11^6]$. Signed $[1]^{12} \ 2-3^8 \ [4]^8 \ 5-9^8 \ 10^4$. Three-piece (medium yellow-green with white shelfback) binding, or medium gray (with bevelled edges) casing—all V cloth (smooth). A white silk ribbon marker is present in some copies. *Locations:* MA, MAJ, WU.

Note: According to the *Independent,* "Twelve thousand copies of the first volume [of Dickinson's poems] . . . have been issued" (46 [14 June 1894], 771), but the *Nation* gives that figure for sales of both *Poems* and *Poems: Second Series* (59 [1 November 1894], 326).

A 1.1.q

Boston: Roberts Brothers, 1895.

'FOURTEENTH EDITION.'. Combined with *Poems: Second Series,* 'EIGHTH EDITION' (see A 2.1.i), in the same manner as A 1.1.o. Gatherings 1 and 11–25 are of thin wove paper; gatherings 2–10 are of calendered paper. Three-piece (medium gray or medium yellow-green shelfbacks with white covers) bindings of V cloth (smooth); a copy has been noted with 'LITTLE · BROWN | AND · COMPANY.' goldstamped at the base of the spine (see *note two*). A white silk ribbon marker is present in some copies. 280 copies printed 18 December 1894. *Locations:* CtY, IEN, JM, MA, NjP, WU.

Note one: Gathering 10, which would normally end with the last page of text in *Poems,* now ends with leaves 7 and 8 containing, respectively, the half title and title leaves for *Poems: Second Series.*

Note two: The copy with the Little, Brown imprint goldstamped on the spine (CtY) was bound after June 1898, when Roberts Brothers was purchased by Little, Brown, and Company.

A 1.1.r

Boston: Roberts Brothers, 1896.

'FIFTEENTH EDITION.'. Collation: $[1-10^8]$. Signed $[1]^{12} \ 2-3^8 \ [4]^8 \ 5-9^8 \ 10^4$. Three-piece (medium yellow-green shelfback with white covers) binding, or medium gray or medium olive (with bevelled edges) casing—all V cloth (smooth). A white silk ribbon marker is present in some copies. 280 copies printed 7 February 1896. Inscribed copy: NjP (10 July 1896). *Locations:* ICN, MAJ, NjP, White.

A 1.1.s

Boston: Roberts Brothers, 1897.

'SIXTEENTH EDITION.'. The advertisement on p. d is now for *Poems, Poems: Second Series, Poems: First and Second Series,* and *Poems: Third Series.* Medium olive (with Roberts Brothers imprint on the spine) or medium gray (with Little, Brown imprint on the spine) casings—both V cloth (smooth) with bevelled edges. A white silk ribbon marker is present in some copies. 280 copies printed 22 March 1897. *Locations:* NN, RPB, White.

Note: The copy with the Little, Brown imprint goldstamped on the spine (NN) was bound after June 1898, when Roberts Brothers was purchased by Little, Brown, and Company.

A 1.1.t

Boston: Little, Brown, and Company, 1898.

'SIXTEENTH EDITION.'. Three-piece (white shelfback with medium olive covers) binding, or medium gray or medium olive (with bevelled edges) casings—all V cloth (smooth) with Little, Brown imprint on the spine. A white silk ribbon marker is present in some copies. Published after June 1898, when Roberts Brothers was purchased by Little, Brown, and Company. *Locations:* JM, MA, MAJ, MWelC, NNC, NjP.

A 1.1.u

Boston: Little, Brown, and Company, 1901.

'SIXTEENTH EDITION.'. Medium gray or medium olive V cloth (smooth) with bevelled edges. A white silk ribbon is present in some copies. WU copy (rebound) received 19 April 1901. *Locations:* JM, MA, NjP, ViU.

A 1.1.v

Boston: Little, Brown, and Company, 1902.

'SIXTEENTH EDITION.'. Dark medium gray or medium olive V cloth (smooth) with bevelled edges. *Locations:* IEN, MA, White.

A 1.1.w

Boston: Little, Brown, and Company, 1904.

'SEVENTEENTH EDITION.'. Medium gray or medium olive V cloth (smooth) with bevelled edges. *Locations:* CtY, ICN, MA, MAJ, RPB.

A 1.1.x
American printing for English sale (1904)

Two issues have been noted:

A 1.1.x$_1$
First issue

POEMS | BY | EMILY DICKINSON | [gothic] Edited by two of her Friends | MABEL LOOMIS TODD AND T. W. HIGGINSON | [flower design] | METHUEN & CO. | 36 ESSEX STREET W.C. | LONDON | 1904

[a–b] [i–iii]; pp. iv–152 are the same as in A 1.1.a.

[1–10^8 $_{(-12)}$] Signed [1]^{11} 2–3^8 [4]^8 5–9^8 [10]^4

Contents: The same as in A 1.1.s, except: pp. c–d (the leaf containing the advertisement for other Dickinson books published by Roberts Brothers) are not present; the copyright page reads 'SEVENTEENTH EDITION.'.

Binding: Deep yellow-green V cloth (calico); front cover: goldstamped single-rule frame; back cover: blank; spine: goldstamped '[rule] | [rule] | POEMS | EMILY | DICKINSON | METHUEN | [rule] | [rule]'. Back laid flyleaf. Laid or laid coated endpapers. Top and front edges trimmed, bottom edges rough-trimmed. Top edges gilded.

Publication: Deposit copy: BL (19 January 1905). Price, 4s.6d.

Locations: BL, MAJ, White.

Note: Like the other American printings of this period, the Methuen *Poems* is on laid paper.

A 1.1.x$_2$
Second issue

POEMS | BY | EMILY DICKINSON | METHUEN & CO. | 36 ESSEX STREET W.C. | LONDON

[a–d] [i–iii]; pp. iv–152 are the same as in A 1.1.a.

[1–10^8 $_{(+12,3)}$] Signed the same as in A 1.1.r. See *note* for an explanation of the cancelled and inserted leaves.

Contents: pp. a–b: blank; p. c: 'POEMS'; p. d: blank; p. i: English title page; p. ii: *'This Edition was First Published in 1905';* pp. iii–152 are the same as in A 1.1.a.

Binding: The same as for the first issue, except: also noted with front and back laid flyleaves; laid endpapers; also noted with top and bottom edges trimmed, front edges rough-trimmed.

Publication: Published January 1905. Price, 4s. 6d.

Locations: MAJ, NjP, RPB, WU.

Note: Leaf 1$_2$ (containing the advertisement for other Dickinson books published by Roberts Brothers) and leaf 1$_3$ (the 1904 English title leaf) have been cancelled; the stubs have been pasted together; and a two-leaf gathering containing the English half title and title leaves has been pasted to the front of the joined stubs.

A 1.1.y

Boston: Little, Brown, and Company, 1906.

'SEVENTEENTH EDITION.'. Three-piece (medium yellow-green shelfback with white covers) binding, or medium gray or medium olive (with bevelled edges) casings—all V cloth (smooth). *Locations:* CSt, MA, NjP, ViU.

A 1.1.z

Boston: Little, Brown, and Company, 1908.

No "edition" designation appears on the copyright page of this or subsequent Little, Brown reprintings. The same contents as in A 1.1.s, except: p. d: blank. Light gray V cloth (smooth) with bevelled edges. *Location:* White.

Note: The following variant between A 1.1.y and A 1.1.z is present:

ii.3–4   [gothic] University Press: | JOHN WILSON AND SON, CAMBRIDGE, U.S.A.
[[gothic] Printers | S. J. PARKHILL & CO., BOSTON, U.S.A.

A 1.1.aa

Boston: Little, Brown, and Company, 1910.

Light gray V cloth (smooth) with front and back covers blank and goldstamping on the spine. *Locations:* MA, MH, NjP, WU, White.

Note: Leaf 1_1 serves as the front pastedown endpaper and leaf 1_2 serves as the front free endpaper.

A 1.1.bb

Boston: Little, Brown, and Company, 1912.

Pagination: [a–b]; pp. i–152 are the same as in A 1.1.a; [153–154]. Collation: $[1–10^8]$. Signed $[1]^{11}$ $2–3^8$ $[4]^8$ $5–9^8$ 10^5. Pp. a–b and 153–154 are blank. Light gray V cloth (smooth) with front and back covers blank and goldstamping on the spine. *Locations:* MA, MAJ, NjP, UU, WU.

A 1.1.cc

Boston: Little, Brown, and Company, 1915.

Wove paper. Light gray or light olive-gray V cloth (smooth) with front and back covers blank and goldstamping on the spine. *Locations:* MAJ, PPT, White.

A 1.1.dd

Boston: Little, Brown, and Company, 1916.

Signed $[1]^{12}$ $2–3^8$ $[4]^8$ $5–9^8$ 10^4. Contents: pp. a–c: blank; p. d: advertisement for *Poems, Poems: Second Series, Poems: First and Second Series,* and *Poems: Third Series;* pp. i–152 are the same as in A 1.1.a. Light gray V cloth (smooth) with front and back covers blank and goldstamping on the spine. Unprinted light yellow-brown paper dust jacket. *Locations:* CtY (dust jacket), MAJ, NjP, White.

A 1.1.ee

Boston: Little, Brown, and Company, 1920.

Light olive gray V cloth (smooth) with front and back covers blank and goldstamping or greenstamping on the spine. *Locations:* IEN, Lowenberg, ViU.

Note: The following variant between A 1.1.dd and A 1.1.ee is present:

ii.3–4   [*printer's imprint*] [[*not present*]

A 1.1.ff

Boston: Little, Brown, and Company, 1922.

Light olive-gray V cloth (smooth) with front and back covers blank and greenstamping on the spine. Inscribed copy: NjP (July 1922). *Locations:* MA, NjP, WU, White.

A 1.1.gg

Boston: Little, Brown, and Company, 1922.

Light olive-gray V cloth (smooth) with front and back covers blank and greenstamping on the spine. *Location:* WU.

Note: The following variant between A 1.1.ff and A 1.1.gg is present:

ii.1–2   *Copyright, 1890,* | BY ROBERTS BROTHERS.   [*Copyright, 1918,* | BY MARTHA
               D. BIANCHI.

A 1.1.hh

Boston: Little, Brown, and Company, 1923.

Light olive-gray V cloth (smooth) with front and back covers blank and greenstamping on the spine. MH copy received 1 May 1924. *Locations:* MH, NN, ScU, White.

Note: Klaus Lubbers reports that 3,820 copies of *Poems* were printed between 1899 and 1925 (*Emily Dickinson: The Critical Revolution* [Ann Arbor: University of Michigan Press, 1968], p. 235).

A 1.1.ii

POEMS | (1890–1896) | BY | EMILY DICKINSON | A FACSIMILE REPRODUCTION | OF THE ORIGINAL VOLUMES | ISSUED IN 1890, 1891, AND 1896 | WITH AN INTRODUC-TION | BY | GEORGE MONTEIRO | *Three volumes in one.* | GAINESVILLE, FLORIDA | SCHOLARS' FACSIMILES & REPRINTS | 1967

Facsimile reprinting of A 1.1.a, combined with *Poems: Second Series* (A 2.1.a) and *Poems: Third Series* (A 4.1.a) in three-volumes-in-one format. Deposit copy: DLC (20 October 1967). Price, $15.00. *Locations:* CtY, DLC, MA, MH, NN, NjP, RPB, ScU, ViU, WU.

A 1.1.jj

FAVORITE | POEMS | of | EMILY DICKINSON | [gothic] Edited by two of her Friends | MABEL LOOMIS TODD AND T. W. HIGGINSON | [gothic] Introduction by | CARY WIL-KINS | [leaf design] | AVENEL BOOKS | NEW YORK

160 pp. Dust jacket. Facsimile reprinting of the fifth or later printing of *Poems* and reprinting of six poems from *Poems: Second Series*. First printing has publisher's code "a" on the copyright page along with 'AVENEL 1978 PRINTING'. Deposit copy: DLC (15 November 1978). Price, $1.98. *Locations:* DLC, JM, White.

Note: Reprintings in cloth, leatherette, or suede have been noted with the following publisher's codes: 'b' (White), 'c' (White), 'f' (JM), 'h' (WU), 'l' (White).

A 1.2
First English edition, only printing (1891)

POEMS

BY

EMILY DICKINSON

EDITED BY TWO OF HER FRIENDS

MABEL LOOMIS TODD AND T. W. HIGGINSON

LONDON

JAMES R. OSGOOD, McILVAINE, & CO.

45, ALBEMARLE STREET

1891

[All rights reserved]

A 1.2: 6⅞″ × 4½″

[a–b] [i–v] vi–viii [ix] x–xiv [15–19] 20–46 [47–48] 49–71 [72–74] 75–112 [113–114] 115–158

[A]⁸ B–I⁸ K⁸

Contents: pp. a–b: blank; p. i: 'POEMS.'; p. ii: blank; p. iii: title page; p. iv: blank; pp. v–viii: 'PREFACE.'; pp. ix–xiv: contents; p. 15: eight lines of verse, the same as in A 1.1.a; p. 16: blank; p. 17: 'I. | [gothic] Life.'; p. 18: blank; pp. 19–46: poems; p. 47: 'II. | [gothic] Love.'; p. 48: blank; pp. 49–71: poems; p. 72: blank; p. 73: 'III. | [gothic] Nature.'; p. 74: blank; pp. 75–112: poems; p. 113: 'IV. | [gothic] Time and Eternity.'; p. 114: blank; pp. 115–158: poems.

Typography and paper: 4³⁄₁₆″ (3⅞″) × 3″; flat calendered paper; 22 lines per page; various lines per page for poetry. Running heads: rectos: p. vii: *'PREFACE.'*; pp. xi–xiii: *'CONTENTS.'*; pp. 21–45, 49–71, 75–111, 115–157: *'POEMS.'*; versos: pp. vi–viii: *'PREFACE.'*; pp. x–xiv: *'CONTENTS.'*; pp. 20–46, 50–70, 76–112, 116–158: *'POEMS.'*.

Binding: Two styles have been noted:

Binding A: Pale yellow V cloth (calico); front cover: goldstamped '[ornate capitals] · POEMS · | [design] | [ornate printing] · Emily · Dickinson · '; back cover: blank; spine: goldstamped '[ornate capitals] POEMS | [Indian pipes] | [two lines in ornate printing] Emily | Dickinson | OSGOOD, | MᶜILVAINE & Cᵒ'. Back laid flyleaf or no flyleaves. Laid endpapers. Top edges trimmed, front and bottom edges rough-trimmed; or all edges trimmed. Top edges gilded.

Binding B: The same as Binding A, except: the last two lines at the base of the spine have been replaced with: goldstamped 'HARPER | AND | BROTHERS' (see *note three*). Coated endpapers. All edges rough-trimmed; or top edges rough-trimmed and front and bottom edges trimmed.

Publication: Listed in the *English Catalogue* for August 1891. Price, 7s. 6d. Deposit copies: Binding A: InU (2 October 1891), BL (9 October 1891), BC (24 February 1892). Inscribed copies: Binding A: MH (15 August 1891), MH (30 September 1891). Mrs. Todd wrote Higginson on 13 August 1891, "I see the *Poems* are just published in London by Osgood," and on 4 December 1891 she wrote in her diary, "Copies of the English edition of Emily's *Poems,* first volume, came" (*Ancestors' Brocades,* p. 155; CtY). According to the *Critic,* "In England, the poems have not been received with any favor" (16 [5 December 1891], 320).

Printing: 'PRINTED BY BALLANTYNE, HANSON AND CO. | EDINBURGH AND LONDON.' (p. 158).

Locations: Binding A: BC, BL, CtY, IEN, InU, MA, MAJ, MB, MH (two copies), NjP, PSt, WU; Binding B: JM, MH.

Note one: The text follows that of A 1.1.e.

Note two: James R. Osgood (of Osgood, McIlvaine) wrote David Todd on 9 October 1891: "Up to the present time we have had no success with the volume of Emily Dickinson's Poems which we brought out here. . . . we do not feel encouraged to venture upon a second volume" (MA).

Note three: Copies in Binding B were bound after June 1897; according to that month's *Publishers' Circular and Booksellers' Record,* "Messrs. Osgood, McIlvaine and Co. have amalgamated their business with that of Messrs. Harper and Brothers, and it will henceforth be carried on by [Harpers]" (66 [26 June 1897], 750).

A 1.3.a
Second American edition, first printing [1948]

EMILY DICKINSON | POEMS FIRST & SECOND SERIES | EDITED BY TWO OF HER FRIENDS | *Mabel Loomis Todd* AND | T. W. HIGGINSON | ILLUSTRATIONS BY *Leon Jacobson* | INTRODUCTION BY *Carl Van Doren* | [drawing of person reclining on grass] | THE WORLD PUBLISHING COMPANY | CLEVELAND AND NEW YORK

256 pp. Dust jacket. *The Living Library L-32*. Price, $1.25. Copyright, 25 June 1948. Deposit copy: DLC (30 July 1948). Publisher's code on copyright page: 'HCI'. *Locations:* CtY, DLC, IEN, JM, MA, MAJ, NcU, NjP, RPB, ViU, WU.

Note: Also noted with publisher's code on copyright page of '2HC853': WU.

A 1.3.b
Second printing [1950]

Cleveland: Fine Editions Press, [1950].

Publisher's code on copyright page: '2WP1053'. Inscribed copy: MAJ (29 December 1950). *Locations:* JM, MAJ, WU.

A 1.3.c
Third printing (1958)

Cleveland and New York: World Publishing Company, 1958.

Wrappers. *The Living Library L-32*. Price, $1.65. *Not seen.*

A2 POEMS: SECOND SERIES

A2.1.a
First edition, first printing (1891)

POEMS

BY

EMILY DICKINSON

Edited by two of her Friends

T. W. HIGGINSON AND MABEL LOOMIS TODD

SECOND SERIES

BOSTON
ROBERTS BROTHERS
1891

A 2.1.a: $6^{7}/_{8}$" $\times$ $4^{1}/_{2}$"

```
┌─────────────────────────────────────────────────────────────┐
│                                                             │
│              Copyright, 1891,                               │
│                                                             │
│           BY ROBERTS BROTHERS.                             │
│                                                             │
│              University Press:                             │
│                                                             │
│       JOHN WILSON AND SON, CAMBRIDGE, U.S.A.               │
│                                                             │
└─────────────────────────────────────────────────────────────┘
```

[i–viii] [1–3] 4–8 [9] 10–16 [17–21] 22–86 [87–89] 90–107 [108–110] 111–177 [178–180] 181–230 [231–232]

[a–b^2] [1]^8 2–14^8 15^4 An unprinted protective tissue is inserted in some copies before the title leaf.

Contents: pp. i–iii: blank; p. iv: advertisement for *Poems* and *Poems: Second Series;* pp. v–viii: facsimile of the manuscript of "Renunciation"; p. 1: title page; p. 2: copyright page; pp. 3–8: 'PREFACE.', signed 'MABEL LOOMIS TODD. | AMHERST, MASSACHUSETTS, | August, 1891.'; pp. 9–16: contents; p. 17: eight lines of verse, beginning 'My nosegays are for captives;'; p. 18: blank; p. 19: 'I. | LIFE.'; p. 20: blank; pp. 21–86: poems; p. 87: 'II. | LOVE.'; p. 88: blank; pp. 89–107: poems; p. 108: blank; p. 109: 'III. | NATURE.'; p. 110: blank; pp. 111–177: poems; p. 178: blank; p. 179: 'IV. | TIME AND ETERNITY.'; p. 180: blank; pp. 181–230: poems; pp. 231–232: blank.

Typography and paper: 4^1⁄$_{16}$″ (3¾″) × 3″; white glossy calendered paper; 23 lines per page; various lines per page for poems. Running heads: rectos: pp. 5–7: 'PREFACE.'; pp. 11–15: 'CONTENTS.'; pp. 23–85, 89–107, 111–177, 181–229: 'POEMS.'; versos: pp. 4–8: 'PREFACE.'; pp. 10–16: 'CONTENTS.'; pp. 22–86, 90–106, 112–176, 182–230: 'POEMS.'.

Binding: Three styles have been noted, priority undetermined:

Binding A: Three-piece binding: medium yellow-green V cloth (smooth) spine, extending over to meet white V cloth (smooth) on front and back covers, the meeting of the two cloths marked by a goldstamped vertical straight rule; front cover: goldstamped '[ornate capitals] · POEMS · | [design] | [two lines in ornate printing] · Emily · Dickinson · | Second Series | [Indian pipes]'; back cover: blank; spine: goldstamped '[ornate capitals] POEMS | [two lines in ornate printing] Second | Series | [Indian pipes] | [two lines in ornate printing] Emily | Dickinson | BOSTON | ROBERTS BROS.'. Front flyleaf; or back flyleaf; or no flyleaves. Wove or coated endpapers. All edges trimmed. All edges gilded. See *note two.*

Binding B: Medium gray or medium olive V cloth (smooth); bevelled edges; front cover: goldstamped '[ornate capitals] · POEMS · | [design] | [two lines in ornate printing] · Emily · Dickinson · | Second Series | [Indian pipes]'; back cover: blank; spine: goldstamped the same as in Binding A. Front flyleaf; coated front flyleaf; back flyleaf; or no flyleaves. Wove or coated endpapers. Top and front edges trimmed, bottom edges rough-trimmed; or all edges trimmed. Top edges gilded.

Binding C: Three-piece three-quarter white leather binding: white leather spine extending over to meet paper-covered boards of black floral patterns on a dark orange-yellow background, the meeting of the two marked by a goldstamped vertical straight rule; front and back covers: white leather outside corners with goldstamped rules where they meet the paper-covered boards; spine: six blindstamped boxes set off with goldstamped rules: boxes 1, 3, 5, and 6 with a goldstamped floral design, box 2 with a dark reddish brown morocco label with goldstamped '[within a single-rule frame] POEMS', and box 4 with a dark reddish brown morocco label with

Binding A for A 2.1.a

goldstamped '[all within a single-rule frame] EMILY | DICKINSON | ** '. Back laid flyleaf; or front and back laid flyleaves. Endpapers of the same design as the paper-covered boards. All edges trimmed. Top edges or all edges gilded. See *note two* and *note three*.

Dust jacket: Unprinted light yellow-brown paper. Probably for Bindings A and B only.

Box: Two-part (slipcase with covering for open end) cardboard box covered with white moiré paper; the slipcase part is fleece-lined. Unprinted. For use with Binding C only; see A 1.1.j, *note two*.

Binding B for A 2.1.a

Publication: 960 copies printed 21 October 1891. Prices: Binding A, $1.50; Binding B, $1.25; Binding C, $3.50.

On 13 July 1891 Mrs. Todd wrote in her diary, "Sending off second volume of E.D.'s poems to Col. Higginson" (CtY). According to Higginson's diary, the final manuscript was sent to Roberts Brothers on 25 July 1891, and he received "the first proof" on 14 August 1891 (*Ancestors' Brocades,* pp. 147, 156). The *Independent* of 3 September 1891 noted, "A new volume of poems, by the late Emily Dickinson, is nearly ready for the press" (43, 1321). On 13 September 1891 Higginson wrote Mrs. Todd that he had returned "the *final* proof," and the next day Mrs. Todd wrote in her diary that she had

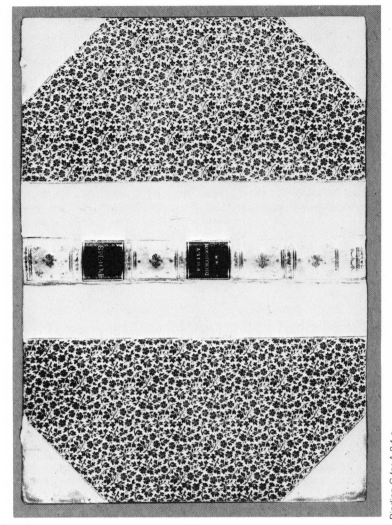

Binding C for A 2.1.a

finished reading "the final proof" (*Ancestors' Brocades,* p. 163; CtY). However, on 5 October 1891 Thomas Niles of Roberts Brothers wrote Mrs. Todd that the printers had the book "on the press" and were holding it up pending receipt of her final corrections (MA). Mrs. Todd wrote in her journal on 18 October 1891 that the book "will be out in a week or so," and on 6 November 1891 she wrote in her diary, "My copies of Emily Dickinson's *Poems,* second volume, came" (*Ancestors' Brocades,* p. 166; CtY).

Bindings A and B advertised in *Publishers' Weekly* 40 (26 September 1891), 451; for 4 November 1891, in *Publishers' Weekly* 40 (24 October 1891), 649; with "Recent Publications," in *Publishers' Weekly* 40 (14 November 1891), 761. Listed in *Publishers' Weekly* 40 (5 December 1891), 879. Deposited for copyright: title, 3 October 1891; book, 5 November 1891. Copyright registration A35536. Copyright renewed 4 January 1919. According to the publisher's records, published 9 November 1891. Deposit copies: Binding B: DLC (5 November 1891), two copies. Inscribed copies: Binding A: CtY (from Mrs. Todd, November 1891), CtY (from Mrs. Todd, 11 November 1891), NjP (13 November 1891), MH (25 December 1891)—two copies, NN (25 December 1891)—two copies, NjP (1 January 1892); Binding B: CtY (from Mrs. Todd, 9 November 1891), PSt (11 November 1891), MA (12 November 1891), RPB (14 December 1891); Binding C: MA (29 February 1892). MBAt copy (Binding B) received 9 November 1891; MB copy (rebound) received 10 November 1891. Royalty, 15% on all copies sold.

Printing: Electrotyped by John Wilson and Son. For printer's imprint, see copyright page illustration.

Locations: Binding A: CtY (two copies) (dust jacket), IEN, MH (two copies), NN (two copies), NjP (two copies), WU; Binding B: CSt, CtY, DLC (two copies), FU, ICN, InU, JM, MA, MBAt, MH, NN, NjP, PSt, RPB, ViU; Binding C: CtY (box), MA, NjP (two copies), WU.

Note one: A white silk ribbon marker is present in some copies.

Note two: Copies of *Poems: Second Series* in the three-piece bindings (Bindings A and C) have had the page edges trimmed more than have those copies in single casings (Binding B); the page size is usually ⅛″ smaller.

Note three: Copies in Binding C have also been bound with gathering a omitted (CtY, WU) or leaf a_1 cancelled (MA, NjP). In all copies, leaf 15_4 has been cancelled. E. D. Hardy of Roberts Brothers wrote David Todd on 9 November 1891 that copies in Binding C had been delayed at the binder's, but he hoped they would be available on the fifteenth or the twentieth (MA).

Note four: Mrs. Todd and Higginson received $100 each for their work on *Poems: Second Series.* According to Mrs. Todd, this was the "last sum of money" she received for working on Emily Dickinson's poetry (*Ancestors' Brocades,* p. 173).

Note five: E. D. Hardy wrote David Todd on 13 November 1891, "The book seems to go like 'Hot Cakes' here also, for our whole Edition with the exception of a few in white & gold [Binding C] have been taken up and we are still behind hand with orders" (MA).

A 2.1.b
Second printing (1892)

Boston: Roberts Brothers, 1892.

Typography and paper: Laid paper with horizontal chain marks 1¾₆″ apart.

Binding: Three styles have been noted, priority undetermined:

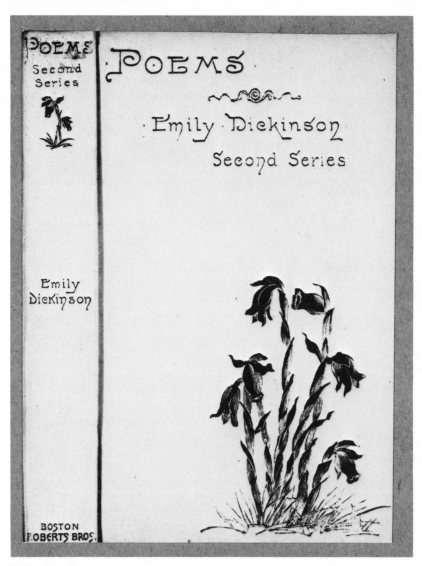

Binding C for A 2.1.b

Binding A: Three-piece binding of medium yellow-green shelfback with white covers—both V cloth (smooth); a copy has been noted with 'LITTLE · BROWN | AND · COMPANY.' goldstamped at the base of the spine (see *note three*).

Binding B: Medium gray or medium olive V cloth (smooth) with bevelled edges.

Binding C: The same as A 2.1.a, Binding B, except: white V cloth (smooth); edges are not bevelled.

Dust jacket: Unprinted light yellow-brown paper.

Box: Two-part (top and bottom) cardboard box covered with calendered paper, except on the insides of both parts and on the bottom of the bottom part. Unprinted. Probably for Binding C only.

Publication: 1,000 copies printed 14 November 1891. Hardy wrote David Todd on 13 November 1891 that a new "edition" had "just gone into the binder's hands" and should be out on the eighteenth (MA). Inscribed copies: Binding B: CtY, JM, MAJ (all 25 December 1891).

Locations: Binding A: MAJ, WU; Binding B: CtY (dust jacket), JM, MA, MAJ, MB, MH, NNC, NcU, NjP, ViU, WU; Binding C: NjP (box).

Note one: A white silk ribbon marker is present in some copies.

Note two: The following textual variants between the first and second printings are present:

29.2	TRIUMPH	[	TRIUMPHANT
29.7	league	[	league—
38.5	Culprit	[	culprit
48.5	blast;	[	blast,
93.9	suspect:	[	suspect,
93.11	Depreciates	[	Depreciate

Note three: The copy with the Little, Brown imprint goldstamped on the spine (MAJ) was bound after June 1898, when Roberts Brothers was purchased by Little, Brown, and Company.

A 2.1.c
Third printing (1892)

Boston: Roberts Brothers, 1892.

Collation: [a–b²] [1]⁸ 2–12⁸ [13]⁸ 14⁸ 15⁴. Three piece (medium yellow-green shelfback with white covers) binding, or medium gray or medium olive (with bevelled edges) casings—all of V cloth (smooth). A white silk ribbon marker is present in some copies. 1,000 copies printed 3 December 1891. *Locations:* JM, MA, NNC, NjP, ViU.

A 2.1.d–e
Fourth and fifth printings (1892)

Boston: Roberts Brothers, 1892.

The copyright page reads 'FOURTH EDITION.'. Three-piece (medium yellow-green shelfback with white covers) binding, or light gray or medium olive (with bevelled edges) casings—both V cloth (smooth), or three-piece three-quarter white leather binding. A white silk ribbon marker is present in some copies. 500 copies printed 22 December 1891; 1,000 copies on 28 December 1891. Inscribed copy: WU (17 April 1892). *Locations:* DLC, JM, MA, MAJ, NjP, RPB, WU.

A 2.1.f
Sixth printing (1893)

Boston: Roberts Brothers, 1893.

'FIFTH EDITION.'. Three-piece (medium yellow-green shelfback with white covers) binding, or medium gray or medium olive (with bevelled edges) casings—all V cloth (smooth). A white silk ribbon marker is present in some copies. *Locations:* ICN, IEN, MA, MAJ, NjP, RPB, WU.

A 2.1.g
Seventh printing (1893)

Boston: Roberts Brothers, 1893.

'SIXTH EDITION.'. Bound with *Poems,* 'ELEVENTH EDITION' (A 1.1.n), in two-volumes-in-one format, See A 1.1.n for further information.

A 2.1.h
Eighth printing (1893)

Boston: Roberts Brothers, 1893.

'SEVENTH EDITION.'. Combined with *Poems,* 'THIRTEENTH EDITION' (A 1.1.o), in two-volumes-in-one format. See A 1.1.o for further information.

Note: According to the *Independent,* "seven thousand [copies] of the second volume" of Dickinson's poems had been "issued" (46 [14 June 1894], 771).

A 2.1.i
Ninth printing (1895)

Boston: Roberts Brothers, 1895.

'EIGHTH EDITION.'. Combined with *Poems,* 'FOURTEENTH EDITION' (A 1.1.q), in two-volumes-in-one format. See A 1.1.q for further information.

A 2.1.j

Boston: Roberts Brothers, 1896.

'NINTH EDITION.'. Collation: $[a-b^2]$ $[1]^8$ $2-9^8$ $[10]^8$ $11-12^8$ $[13]^8$ 14^8 15^4. Contents: the same as in A 2.1.a, except: p. iii: 'POEMS | BY | EMILY DICKINSON. | [rule] | SECOND SERIES.'; p. iv: advertisement for *Poems, Poems: Second Series, Poems: First and Second Series,* and *Poems: Third Series.* Medium gray or medium olive V cloth (smooth) with bevelled edges. A white silk ribbon marker is present in some copies. 280 copies printed 9 October 1896. *Locations:* MA, MAJ, NjP, White.

A 2.1.k

Boston: Little, Brown, and Company, 1898.

'TENTH EDITION.'. Collation: $[a-b^2]$ $[1]^8$ $2-5^8$ $[6-7^8]$ $8-9^8$ $[10]^8$ $11-12^8$ $[13]^8$ 14^8 15^4. Medium gray or medium olive V cloth (smooth) with bevelled edges, with either Roberts Brothers or Little, Brown imprint goldstamped at the base of the spine. A white silk ribbon marker is present in some copies. Published after June 1898, when Roberts Brothers was purchased by Little, Brown, and Company. *Locations:* IEG, JM, MA, MAJ, NjP.

A 2.1.l

Boston: Little, Brown, and Company, 1901.

'TENTH EDITION.'. Three-piece (medium yellow-green shelfback with white covers) binding, or medium gray or medium olive (with bevelled edges) casings—all V cloth (smooth). RPB copy received 19 December 1901. *Locations:* CU-SD, MAJ, NjP, RPB, White.

A 2.1.m

Boston: Little, Brown, and Company, 1904.

'TENTH EDITION.'. The manuscript facsimile is on wove paper. Three-piece (medium yellow-green shelfback with white covers) binding, or medium gray or medium olive (with bevelled edges) casings—all V cloth (smooth). Inscribed copy: CtY (8 March 1905). *Locations:* CSt, CtY, JM, MAJ, NjP.

A 2.1.n

Boston: Little, Brown, and Company, 1906.

'TENTH EDITION.'. Three-piece binding of medium yellow-green shelfback with white covers—both V cloth (smooth). *Locations:* NjP, ViU.

A 2.1.o

Boston: Little, Brown, and Company, 1910.

No "edition" designation appears on the copyright page of this and subsequent Little, Brown reprintings. Medium gray V cloth (smooth) with bevelled edges; or light gray or medium gray V cloth (smooth) with front and back covers blank and goldstamping on the spine. *Locations:* JM, MA, MAJ, NjP, WU.

Note: The following variant between A 2.1.n and A 2.1.o is present:

2.3–4   [gothic] University Press: | John Wilson and Son. Cambridge, U.S.A.
[[gothic] Printers | S. J. Parkhill & Co., Boston, U.S.A.

A 2.1.p

Boston: Little, Brown, and Company, 1913.

Light gray V cloth (smooth) with front and back covers blank and goldstamping on the spine. *Locations:* MA, MAJ, NjP, White.

A 2.1.q

Boston: Little, Brown, and Company, 1916.

Pagination: [i–ii]; pp. 1–230 are the same as in A 2.1.a. Collation: [1–14^8 15^8]. Signed [1]^9 2–5^8 [6–7^8] 8–9^8 [10]^8 11–12^8 [13]^8 14^8 15^3; a two-leaf gathering of wove paper with a manuscript facsimile is inserted after leaf 1$_1$. Contents: pp. i–ii are the same as pp. iii–iv in A 2.1.k; pp. 1–230 are the same as in A 2.1.a. Wove paper. Light gray or medium olive gray V cloth (smooth) with front and back covers blank and goldstamping on the spine. Dust jacket of unprinted light yellow-brown paper. *Locations:* CtY (dust jacket), MAJ, NcU, NjP.

A 2.1.r

Boston: Little, Brown, and Company, 1920.

Pagination: [i–iv]; pp. 1–232 are the same as in A 2.1.a. Collation: [a]^8 [1]^2 2–5^8 [6–7^8] 8–9^8 [10]^8 11–12^8 [13]^8 14^8 15^4; a two-leaf gathering of thin wove paper with a manuscript facsimile is inserted after leaf a$_2$. Contents: pp. i–iv are the same as in A 2.1.j; pp. 1–232 are the same as in A 2.1.a. Light gray or light olive-gray V cloth (smooth) with front and back covers blank and goldstamping or greenstamping on the spine. *Locations:* IEN, NjP, ViU.

Note: The following variants between A 2.1.q and A 2.1.r are present:

2.1–2   *Copyright, 1891,* | By Roberts Brothers.   [*Copyright, 1919,* | By Martha
           Dickinson Bianchi.
2.3–4   [*printer's imprint*]   [[*not present*]

A 2.1.s

Boston: Little, Brown, and Company, 1923.

Contents: [i–iv]; pp. 1–230 are the same as in A 2.1.a; [231–236]. Collation: [1–15^8].
Signed [1]^{10} [2]^8 3–5^8 [6–7^8] 8–9^8 [10]^8 11–12^8 [13]^8 14^8 15^6; a two-leaf gathering of
wove paper with a manuscript facsimile is inserted after leaf a$_2$. Contents: pp. i–ii:
blank; p. iii: half title; p. iv: blank; pp. 1–230 are the same as in A 2.1.a; pp. 231–236:
blank. Light olive-gray V cloth (smooth) with front and back covers blank and gold-
stamping or greenstamping on the spine. MH copy received 17 April 1924. *Locations:*
MA, MH, NN, NjP, WU.

Note: Klaus Lubbers estimates the total sales of *Poems: Second Series* at 7,500
copies (*Emily Dickinson: The Critical Revolution* [Ann Arbor: University of Michigan
Press, 1968], p. 238).

A 2.1.u

Gainesville, Fla.: Scholars' Facsimiles & Reprints, 1967.

Facsimile reprinting of A 2.1.a, combined with *Poems* (A 1.1.a) and *Poems: Third
Series* (A 4.1.a) in three-volumes-in-one format; see A 1.1.ii for further information.·

A 2.2.a
Second edition, first printing (1948)

Cleveland: World Publishing Company, 1948.

See A 1.3.a for further information.

A 2.2.b
Second printing [1950]

Cleveland: Fine Editions Press, [1950].

See A 1.3.b for further information.

A 2.2.c
Third printing (1958)

Cleveland: World Publishing Company, 1968.

See A 1.3.c for further information.

A 3 LETTERS OF EMILY DICKINSON

A 3.1.a
First edition, first printing (1894)

LETTERS

OF

EMILY DICKINSON

EDITED BY

MABEL LOOMIS TODD

IN TWO VOLUMES

VOLUME I

BOSTON
ROBERTS BROTHERS
1894

A 3.1.a: 6¹³/₁₆″ × 4⅜″

Copyright, 1894

By ROBERTS BROTHERS

University Press

JOHN WILSON AND SON, CAMBRIDGE, U.S.A.

Vol. I: [i–iv] [i–v] vi–xii [1] 2–64 [65] 66–124 [125] 126–154 [155] 156–158 [159] 160–188 [189] 190–217 [218] 219–228

Vol. II: [i–v] vi [vii–viii] [229] 230–299 [300] 301–331 [332] 333–354 [355] 356–365 [366] 367–429 [430] 431–441 [442–443] 444–454 [455–456]

Vol. I: [a–b^2] [c^4] 1–14^8 15^2 Inserted frontispiece after leaf a$_1$

Vol. II: [a^4] 1–14^8 15^2 Inserted frontispiece after leaf a$_1$

Contents: Vol. I: p. i: 'LETTERS | OF | EMILY DICKINSON | VOL. I.'; p. ii: blank; inserted frontispiece of stiff wove paper with a portrait of Dickinson as a child printed on the verso, followed by an unprinted protective tissue; p. iii: title page; p. iv: copyright page; p. i: contents; p. ii: blank; p. iii: 'LIST OF ILLUSTRATIONS'; p. iv: blank; pp. v–xii: 'INTRODUCTORY', signed 'MABEL LOOMIS TODD | AMHERST, MASSACHUSETTS | *October* 1894'; pp. 1–158: texts of letters; p. 159: facsimile of manuscript letter; pp. 160–217: texts of letters; p. 218: facsimile of manuscript letter; pp. 219–228: texts of letters; Vol. II: p. i: half title, the same as in Vol. I, except 'II.'; p. ii: blank; inserted frontispiece on calendered paper with a photograph of Dickinson's home printed on the verso, followed by an unprinted protective tissue; p. iii: title page, the same as in Vol I, except 'II.'; p. iv: copyright page, the same as in Vol. I; pp. v–vi: contents; p. vii: 'LIST OF ILLUSTRATIONS"; p. viii: blank; pp. 229–354: texts of letters; p. 355: facsimile of manuscript letter; pp. 356–441: texts of letters; p. 442: blank; pp. 443–454: 'INDEX'; pp. 455–456: blank.

Typography and paper: 5¼″ (4^{15}⁄₁₆″) × 2^{15}⁄₁₆″; laid paper with horizontal chain marks 1³⁄₁₆″ apart; 30 lines per page. Running heads: Vol. I: rectos: pp. vii–xi: '*INTRODUC-TORY*'; pp. 1–63, 67–123, 127–153, 157, 161–187, 191–227: '*LETTERS OF EMILY DICKINSON* [open bracket with year of letter]'; versos: pp. vi–xii: '*INTRODUCTORY*'; pp. 2–216, 220–228: '[year of letter with closed bracket] *TO* [name of recipient]'; Vol. II: rectos: pp. 231–353, 357–441: '*LETTERS OF EMILY DICKINSON* [open bracket with year of letter]'; pp. 445–453: '*INDEX*'; versos: p. vi: '*CONTENTS*'; pp. 230–298, 302–330, 334–364, 368–428, 432–440: '[year of letter with closed bracket] *TO* [name of recipient]'; pp. 444–454: '*INDEX*'.

Binding: Medium yellowish green buckram; front cover: goldstamped Indian pipes; back cover: blank; spine: goldstamped 'EMILY | DICKINSON'S | LETTERS | [one Indian pipe] [two Indian pipes] | BOSTON | ROBERTS BROS.'. Laid front flyleaf in Vol. II. Wove endpapers. All edges trimmed.

Dust jacket: Very light yellow-brown laid paper; front cover: the same as the front cover of the binding, but in black; back cover: blank; spine: the same as the spine of the binding, but in black; front and back flaps: blank.

Box: Unprinted light yellowish green coated paper-covered cardboard box open at one end; spine: brown leather label with goldstamped 'EMILY | DICKINSON'S | LET-TERS'; green silk ribbon marker attached to the box.

Publication: 1,000 copies of Vol. I printed 29 October 1894; 1,000 copies of Vol. II printed 14 November 1894. Price, $2.00 a set.

Austin Dickinson wrote E. D. Hardy of Roberts Brothers on 26 September 1894 that his sister Lavinia had agreed to the following terms: the copyright was to be in Lavinia's name; Lavinia would pay for and retain the plates; and a 15% royalty would be split equally between Lavinia and Mrs. Todd (MA). The contract states that a 15% royalty was to be paid to both women only after the plates had been paid for; in other words, neither Lavinia nor Mrs. Todd were to receive cash payments until after their 15% royalty had covered the costs of making the plates (photostat, CtY, and see *note four* below). Apparently 2,000 sets had to be sold before the plates were paid for.

Mrs. Todd wrote Thomas Niles of Roberts Brothers on 21 August 1893 that she hoped to begin sending him copy "in a few days" (MA). Mrs. Todd wrote Niles on 26 February 1894, "The *Letters* are going to be a good deal larger than we thought. . . . Now, it has occurred to me to ask whether it would not do to have two small volumes, say of 250 pages each, instead of one with the 500 which it seems to be growing into. . . . I do not believe it can make less than 500 pages" (MA). Mrs. Bingham states that "proof reading was under way" by 9 January 1894 (*Ancestors' Brocades,* p. 267). Proofing took longer than usual because Mrs. Todd sent proofs to each of Emily Dickinson's correspondents who had allowed her letters to them to be used, permitting them to check for accuracy and to make any revisions they deemed necessary. On 24 September 1894 Mrs. Todd wrote in her diary, "Everything now in the printer's hands except *Index* and *Contents*" (CtY). Mrs. Todd's diary shows that "complete plate proofs" of both volumes arrived on 5 November, and that she worked until the afternoon of 7 November to finish checking them (CtY). And on 21 November 1894, Mrs. Todd wrote in her diary, "The E.D. *Letters* came today . . . the two volumes in a box" (CtY).

Advertised for September 1894 in *Publishers' Weekly* 46 (1 September 1894), 270. Incorrectly noted as "just ready" in *Publishers' Weekly* 46 (1 September 1894), 271. Noted for 10 November 1894 in the *Nation* 59 (1 November 1894), 325. Advertised for 15 November 1894 in *Publishers' Weekly* 46 (3 November 1894), 670, and in a Roberts Brothers trade flyer (CtY). Listed in *Publishers' Weekly* 46 (8 December 1894), 1002. Deposited for copyright: title, 13 October 1894; book, 21 November 1894. Copyright registrations A47754, A47755. According to the publisher's records, published 15 November 1894. Deposit copy: DLC (21 November 1894). Inscribed copies: NNC (from Lavinia Dickinson, 29 November 1894), MA (from Mrs. Todd, 3 December 1894), MA (from Mrs. Todd, 8 December 1894), ViU (25 December 1894). MBAt copy received 27 November 1894; MH copy received 14 December 1894; Boston Library Society copy (now at MH) received 18 December 1894. Royalty, 15% on all copies sold. Listed in the *English Catalogue* as an importation for December 1894 at 9s. a set.

Printing: Electrotyped by John Wilson and Son. For printer's imprint, see the copyright page illustration.

Locations: CtY, DLC, ICN, IEN, InU, JM (II), Lowenberg (box), MA (two copies) (dust jacket), MAJ (dust jacket, partial box), MB, MBAt, MH (two copies), NN, NNC, NcU, NjP, PSt, ViU (dust jacket, partial box), WU.

Note one: A copy of Vol. I of the first printing sheets bound in a second printing, Binding B, casing, apparently a binding oddity of no significance, has been noted: WU.

Note two: An unbound, sewn set of folded and gathered signatures (measuring 7" × 4½", with all edges rough-trimmed, a two-leaf gathering of stiff paper at the front and back of each volume, and a front flyleaf of laid paper in Vol. II) has been noted: CtY.

Note three: Mrs. Todd wrote in her diary on 27 November 1894, "First edition (1000) of *Letters* all sold," but on 11 December 1894 Hardy wrote Mrs. Todd, "So far we have not sold all of the 1ˢᵗ Edition but they may go this week" (CtY; MA).

Note four: Mrs. Bingham notes that since "receipts from sales had amounted to little more than enough to pay for the plates, the equal division of royalties between sister [Lavinia] and editor [Mrs. Todd] had been an empty compact. No income from that book ever materialized for either of them" (*Ancestors' Brocades,* p. 338).

A 3.1.b
Second Printing (1894)

Two issues have been noted:

A 3.1.b₁
First issue (1894)

Boston: Roberts Brothers, 1894.

Vol. I: [i–v] vi–xii [xiii–xvi]; pp. 1–228 are the same as in the first printing

Vol. II: The same as in the first printing

Vol. I: [1]⁸ 1–14⁸ 15²

Vol. II: The same as in the first printing

Contents: Vol. I: pp. i–xii: the same as pp. i–iv (beginning with the half title) and pp. v–xii of the first printing; pp. xiii–xvi: the same as pp. i–iv (beginning with the contents) of the first printing; pp. 1–228: the same as in the first printing; Vol. II: the same as in the first printing.

Typography and paper: The same as in the first printing.

Binding: Five styles have been noted: Bindings A and B are earliest, Binding E is latest; priority of Bindings A and B and Bindings C and D undetermined:

Binding A: The same as the first printing binding, except: no flyleaves; laid end-papers.

Binding B: Deep brown V cloth (smooth); front and back covers: blank; spine: silverstamped the same as in the first printing binding, except: at the base of the spine is 'ROBERTS | BROTHERS | BOSTON'. Laid flyleaves. Laid endpapers. All edges trimmed.

Binding C: The same as Binding A, except: goldstamped 'LITTLE · BROWN | AND · COMPANY.' at the base of the spine; no flyleaves; laid endpapers.

Binding D: The same as Binding C, except: the pubisher's name on the spines and the Indian pipes on the front covers of both volumes are blackstamped; no flyleaves; laid endpapers.

Binding E: Bound in two-volumes-in-one format in medium yellowish brown V cloth (smooth); front and back covers: blank; spine: white paper label with '[all within a single-rule frame] THE LETTERS | OF | EMILY | DICKINSON | [rule] | 1845–1886'. Laid or wove endpapers. Top edges trimmed, front and bottom edges rough-trimmed; top and bottom edges trimmed, front edges rough-trimmed; or all edges trimmed.

Dust jacket: The same as the first printing dust jacket.

Publication: 1,500 copies of Vol. I printed 8 December 1894; 1,500 copies of Vol. II printed 10 December 1894. Mrs. Todd sent a "list of corrections" for the second printing to E. D. Hardy of Roberts Brothers on 28 November 1894 (MA). Hardy wrote Mrs. Todd on 11 December 1894, "The second Edition will be ready in a few days" (MA).

Locations: Binding A: CtY (dust jacket), FU, JM, MA, NNC, NjP; Binding B: CtY, MA, MAJ, NjP, WU (II); Binding C: CSt, JM, MA, NjP; Binding D: MA, NjP, RPB; Binding E: CU-SD, CtY, JM, MA, MAJ, MH, NNC, NcU, NjP, PSt, RPB, ViU, WU.

Note one: Copies with the Little, Brown imprint stamped on the spine (Bindings C and D) were bound after June 1898, when Roberts Brothers was purchased by Little, Brown, and Company.

Note two: Klaus Lubbers reports that "1200 [copies of *Letters*] were still unsold in 1898" (*Emily Dickinson: The Critical Revolution* [Ann Arbor: University of Michigan Press, 1968], p. 240).

Note three: The following variants between the first and second printings are present:

I.i.4	VOL. [VOLUME
I.i–xii	["Table of Contents" and "List of Illustrations" are before "Introductory"] [I.v–xvi ["Introductory" is before "Table of Contents" and "List of Illustrations"]
I.iii.3	DICKINSON · · *Frontispiece* [I.xv.3 DICKINSON · *Frontispiece*
I.v.4–6	for her prose that her sister | has gathered these letters, and committed their pre- | paration to me. [for some of her prose that | her sister has asked me to prepare these volumes | of her letters.
I.132.28–29	etc.' | [blank] [etc.'—*Poems,* | First Series, page 74.
I.142.21	*Ford.* [*Ford*
I.146.22	*Anthon.* [*Anthon*
I.147.20	*Same.* [*Same*
I.148.1	*Same.* [*Same*
I.149.15	*Same.* [*Same*
I.152.10	*Same.* [*Same*
I.153.6	*Same.* [*Same*
I.153.20	*Same.* [*Same*
I.155.2	*Holland.* [*Holland*
I.228.17	VOL. [VOLUME
II.i.4	VOL. [VOLUME
II.229.4	[boldface italic 'T'] [[italic 'T']
II.370.9	*Flowers* [*Flowers*[2]
II.370.9	*Morning.* [*Morning.*[3]
II.370.27	[note one begins under the space after 'soar' in the line above] [[note one begins under 'So' in the line above]
II.370.28–29	[blank] [[2] *Poems,* Second Series, page 122. | [3] Ibid., page 113.
II.439.13	[ ]ty [ity
II.444.col.1.23	Bramwell [Branwell
II.446.col.1.2	67 [67, 298
II.446.col.1.3	182 [182, 282
II.446.col.2.42	174 [174, 290, 349
II.447.col.1.9	'Give me thine heart,' 395 [Gladstone, 293
II.447.col.1.11	x [ix

Note four: There exists some confusion over the number of copies printed with the first printing reading at I.v.4–6. In the first printing, this reading indicates that Lavinia had much more to do with the editing of *Letters* than she actually did, an impression corrected in the second printing reading. According to Mrs. Bingham, Lavinia saw proofs containing the second printing reading, complained, and Mrs. Todd instructed the printer to revise the statement back to the first printing reading. But Austin Dickinson "would not allow the proof to stand as corrected," and ordered the printer to run off only ten copies containing Lavinia's desired reading. Mrs. Bingham concludes that this resulted in giving "an added collector's value to the few differing copies, the exact number of which I have been unable to verify" (*Ancestors' Brocades,* pp. 304–305). Given the number of copies located with the "Lavinia reading," it is impossible that only ten were printed thus. Because no copies have been located containing the "Lavinia reading" of the first printing together with the second printing readings at all the other points, it seems likely that the "Lavinia reading" was present in all copies of the first printing and changed for all copies of the second printing.

A 3.1.b₂
Second issue (1906)

The Letters | of | Emily Dickinson | 1845–1886 | Edited by | Mabel Loomis Todd | *With a Portrait of Emily Dickinson, a View of* | *her Home, and Facsimiles* | Boston | Little, Brown, and Company | 1906

[a⁸ ₍₊ₐ₂₎] 1–14⁸ 15² [a⁴ ₍₋ₐ₂₎] 1–14⁸ 15². Bound in two-volumes-in-one format. The Roberts Brothers title leaf has been cancelled in both volumes, with a cancel Little, Brown, and Company title leaf inserted at the beginning of Vol. I only; pagination and contents are affected accordingly.

Binding: The same as the second printing, first issue, Binding E, except: top edges trimmed, front and bottom edges rough-trimmed; top edges gilded; laid endpapers.

Publication: Advertised as a "new edition" in *Publishers' Weekly* 70 (29 September 1906), 883. Listed in *Publishers' Weekly* 70 (15 September 1906), 564. Price, $1.25. Inscribed copy: CtY (November 1906).

Locations: CtY, MA, MAJ, NjP, RPB, ViU.

A 3.2.a
Second edition, first printing (1931)

LETTERS

OF

EMILY DICKINSON

EDITED BY

Mabel Loomis Todd

NEW AND ENLARGED EDITION

HARPER & BROTHERS PUBLISHERS
NEW YORK AND LONDON
1 9 3 1

A 3.2.a: 8⅝″ × 5⅝″; Dickinson's name, the publisher's logo, and the date are in medium green

```
┌─────────────────────────────────────────────────────┐
│                   LETTERS                            │
│                     OF                               │
│              EMILY DICKINSON                         │
│            ──────────────────────                    │
│            Copyright, 1931, by                       │
│      Millicent Bingham and Mabel Loomis Todd         │
│          Printed in the United States                │
│            ──────────────────────                    │
│                FIRST EDITION                         │
│                    I-F                               │
│  All rights in this book are reserved.               │
│  No part of the text may be reproduced in any        │
│  manner whatsoever without permission in             │
│       writing from Harper & Brothers.                │
└─────────────────────────────────────────────────────┘
```

[i–v] vi–vii [viii] ix–xi [xii] xiii–xxxi [xxxii–xxxiv] 1–188 [188a–188b] 189–348 [348a–348b] 349–431 [432] 433–457 [458] The pages designated 188a–188b and 348a–348b contain facsimiles of manuscript letters

[1–31⁸] Inserted leaves of coated paper containing illustrations are placed before the title page and between pp. xvi–xvii, 24–25, 52–53, 62–63, 80–81, 148–149, 154–155, 182–183, 214–215, 224–225, 254–255, 282–283, 290–291, 418–419, and 439–440

Contents: p. i: '*LETTERS* | OF | EMILY DICKINSON | [rule] | [rule] | [flower]'; p. ii: blank; inserted leaf of coated paper with a sepia photograph of Dickinson printed on the verso; p. iii: title page; p. iv: copyright page; pp. v–vi: contents; p. vii: list of illustrations; p. viii: blank; pp. ix–xi: '*PREFACE*', signed 'MABEL LOOMIS TODD. | *Coconut Grove, Florida* | April, 1931'; p. xii: blank; pp. xiii–xxiv: 'INTRODUCTION TO SECOND EDITION', signed the same as the "Preface" [a leaf of coated paper with facsimiles of Dickinson's handwriting printed in sepia on both sides is inserted after p. xvi]; pp. xxv–xxxi: 'INTRODUCTION TO FIRST EDITION', signed 'MABEL LOOMIS TODD. | Amherst, Massachusetts | October, 1894'; p. xxxii: blank; p. xxxiii: '*LETTERS* | OF | EMILY DICKINSON'; p. xxxiv: blank; pp. 1–56: texts of letters to Mrs. A. R. Strong [a foldout leaf of text paper with a facsimile of a manuscript letter printed on the recto is inserted after p. 22; a leaf of coated paper with sepia photographs of Dickinson's home and the Mount Holyoke Seminary printed on the recto is inserted after p. 24; a leaf of coated paper with a sepia photograph of Abiah Root Strong printed on the recto is inserted after p. 52]; pp. 57–61: texts of letters to Joel Warren Norcross; pp. 62–122: texts of letters to William Austin Dickinson [a leaf of coated paper with a sepia photograph of William Austin Dickinson printed on the recto is inserted after p. 62; an inserted leaf of coated paper with a sepia photograph of Jenny Lind and Otto Goldschmidt printed on the recto is inserted after p. 80]; pp. 123–152: texts of letters to Mrs. Gordon L. Ford, Mr. Bowdoin, Mrs. Kate Anthon, and Lavinia Dickinson [a leaf of coated paper with a sepia photograph of Lavinia Dickinson printed on the recto is inserted after p. 148]; pp. 153–180: texts of letters to Dr. and Mrs. J. G. Holland [a leaf of coated paper with a sepia photograph of Dr. Holland printed on the recto is inserted after p. 154]; pp. 181–213: texts of letters to Samuel and Mrs. Bowles [a leaf of coated paper with a sepia photograph of Samuel Bowles printed on the recto is inserted after p. 182; a facsimile of a manuscript letter is on pp. 188a–188b]; pp. 214–270: texts of letters to Louisa and Frances Lavinia Norcross [a leaf of coated paper with a sepia photograph of Emily Dickinson's home printed on the recto is inserted after p. 214; a leaf of coated paper with a sepia photograph of Frazer A. Stearns printed on the recto is inserted after p. 224; a leaf of coated paper with a sepia photograph of Edward Dickinson printed on the recto is inserted after p. 254]; pp. 271–321: texts of letters to Thomas Wentworth Higginson [a leaf of coated paper with a sepia photograph of a manuscript letter to Higginson printed on the recto is inserted after p. 282; a leaf of coated paper with a sepia photograph of Higginson printed on the recto is inserted after p. 290]; pp. 322–341: texts of letters to Perez D. Cowan, Maria Whitney, Samuel Bowles, Elizabeth Hoar, and Mr. and Mrs. Rockwood Hoar; pp. 342–357: texts of letters to James D. Clark and Charles H. Clark [a facsimile of a manuscript letter is on pp. 348a–348b]; pp. 358–391: texts of letters to Mr. and Mrs. J. L. Jenkins, Mrs. Hanson Read, Mrs. W. A. Stearns, Mrs. Edward Tuckerman, Mrs. J. S. Cooper, Mrs. A. B. H. Davis, Mrs. H. F. Hills, Mrs. Jameson, and Maggie Maher; pp. 392–417: texts of letters to the Rev. F. F. Emerson, Mr. and Mrs. George Montague, Mrs. W. F. Stearns, Mr. and Mrs. Joseph A. Sweetser, Mrs. J. K. Chickering, Thomas Niles, Mrs. Carmichael, Dr. and Mrs. Thomas P. Field, Theodore Holland, "H. H." [Helen Hunt Jackson], Mrs. E. P. Crowell, Eugenia Hall, and J. C. Greenough; pp. 418–431: texts of letters to Mrs. Mabel Loomis Todd, Mr. and Mrs. E. J. Loomis, Mrs. Edward Tuckerman, the Misses Norcross, C. H. Clark, and Mrs. Elizabeth Dickinson Currier [a leaf of coated paper with a sepia photograph of Mabel Loomis Todd printed on the recto is inserted after p. 418]; p. 432: blank; pp. 433–439: 'APPENDIX I' ["Passages Omitted from the First (1894) Edition of Emily Dickinson's Letters, Inserted in This, Second, Edition"]; pp. 440–442: 'APPENDIX II' ["Parents and Brothers and Sisters of Edward Dickinson, Emily's Father," "Parents and Brothers and Sisters of Emily Norcross Dickinson, Emily's Mother," and "Dates of Importance in the Life of Emily Dickinson"] [a leaf of coated paper with sepia photographs of Joel Norcross Dickinson printed on the recto and Mrs. Joel Norcross Dickinson printed on the verso is inserted after p. 440]; pp. 443–444: 'APPENDIX III' ["Poems Sent to Colonel Higginson by Emily Dickinson in Addition to Those Included in the Text of Her Letters to Him"]; pp. 445–454: "Index"; pp. 455–457: "First Lines of Poems Included in the Text of Letters"; p. 458: blank.

Typography and paper: 5¹⁵⁄₁₆″ (5¾″) × 3⅝″; laid paper with vertical chain marks ¹¹⁄₁₆″ apart; 31 lines per page. Running heads: rectos: p. xi: 'PREFACE'; pp. xv–xxiii: 'INTRODUCTION TO SECOND EDITION'; pp. xxvii–xxxi: 'INTRODUCTION TO FIRST EDITION'; pp. 3–55, 59–121, 125–151, 155–179, 183–269, 273–431: '[year]] To [name of recipient]'; pp. 285–287: '[1870] LETTER OF COL. T. W. HIGGINSON'; pp. 341, 343, 359, 431: '[year] LETTERS OF EMILY DICKINSON'; pp. 435–441: 'APPENDICES'; pp. 447–453: 'INDEX'; p. 457: 'FIRST LINES OF POEMS'; versos: p. vi: 'CONTENTS'; p. x: 'PREFACE'; pp. xiv–xxiv: 'INTRODUCTION TO SECOND EDITION'; pp. xxvi–xxx: 'INTRODUCTION TO FIRST EDITION'; pp. 2–60, 64–212, 216–320, 324–340, 344–356, 360–390, 394–416, 420–430: 'LETTERS OF EMILY DICKINSON [[year]'; pp. 434–438, 442–444: 'APPENDICES'; pp. 446–454: 'INDEX'; pp. 456: 'INDEX TO FIRST LINES'.

Binding: Dark yellowish green V cloth (smooth); front cover: goldstamped 'LETTERS OF EMILY DICKINSON | [Indian pipes at bottom right]'; back cover: blank; spine: goldstamped *'LETTERS* | OF | EMILY | DICKINSON | [design] | EDITED BY | Mabel Loomis | Todd | HARPERS'. Wove endpapers watermarked '[curved] WARREN'S | OLDE STYLE'. Top and bottom edges trimmed, front edges rough-trimmed, or all edges trimmed.

Dust jacket: Light pink paper; front cover: 'EMILY DICKINSON SELF-REVEALED | [three lines in green] *LETTERS* | OF | EMILY DICKINSON | [rule] | [rule] | EDITED BY |

Mabel Loomis Todd | [22-line blurb for the book] | [rule] | [rule] | [green] *Harper & Brothers Publishers* | ESTABLISHED 1817'; back cover: advertisements for five Harper titles in biography; spine: '[rule] | [rule] | [four lines in green] *LETTERS* | OF | EMILY | DICKINSON | *Edited by* | Mabel Loomis | Todd | [rule] | [rule] | [17-line blurb by Louis Untermeyer] | [rule] | [rule] | [green] HARPERS'; front flap: description of the book; back flap: blurbs for *The Life and Letters of Sir Edmund Gosse*.

Publication: 1,425 copies printed. The publisher's code ('I-F') indicates September 1931 printing. Price, $4.00.

A. W. Rushmore of Harper wrote Mrs. Bingham on 16 June 1931 that castoffs had "come to hand" (CtY). On 21 September 1931, E. F. Saxton of Harper wrote Mrs. Bingham that "a set of proofs" was available (CtY). The contract between Harper and Mrs. Todd and Mrs. Bingham called for a 10% royalty to be paid on the first 3,000 copies sold, a 12½% royalty on the next 3,000 copies sold, and a 15% royalty on all additional copies sold (CtY).

Advertised for $5.00 in *Publishers' Weekly* 120 (19 September 1931), 1158. Copyright application received, 17 November 1931; books received, 3 November 1931. Copyright registration A43826. Copyright renewed, 27 May 1959. According to the publisher's records, published 4 November 1931. Deposit copy: DLC (3 November 1931), two copies. Inscribed copy: MA (from the editors, October 1931). NN copy (rebound) received from the publisher 22 October 1931; MBAt copy received 2 November 1931; RPB copy received 3 November 1931. Royalty, 10% of the first 3,000 copies sold, 12½% on the next 3,000 copies sold, 15% on all additional copies sold.

Printing: Printed and bound by the Haddon Press, Haddon, Pa.

Locations: CtY (dust jacket), DLC, ICN, JM (dust jacket), MA (dust jacket), MAJ (dust jacket), MB (dust jacket), MBAt, MH, NjP (dust jacket), PSt (dust jacket), RPB (dust jacket), WU.

Note: Distributed in England by Hamish Hamilton, who cut the American price off the front flap of the dust jacket and stamped there the English price of 12s. 6d; this is the only difference between copies sold in America and England (copy at MAJ, received 8 December 1931). Published late November 1931. 150 copies sent to England, of which 45 had been sold by 30 June 1932 (see A. Flashner, 19 November 1931, and Harper, 30 June 1932, to Mrs. Bingham, CtY).

A3.2.b
Second edition, second printing (1931)

New York: Harper & Brothers, 1931.

Dickinson's name, the publisher's logo, and the date are in green. The copyright page reads 'SECOND PRINTING | L-F'; the publisher's code indicates November 1931 printing. 750 copies printed. NjP copy received 20 November 1931. *Locations:* MA, MAJ, NjP, White.

Note: A. Flashner of Harper wrote Mrs. Bingham on 19 November 1931, "Copies of the second printing have just come in" (CtY).

A3.2.c
Second edition, third printing [1932]

New York: Harper & Brothers, [1932].

The title page is all in black. The copyright page reads "THIRD PRINTING | K-G'; the publisher's code indicates October 1932 printing. *Locations:* CSt, NcD.

A 3.3.a
Third edition, first American printing [1951]

[seven lines within a single-rule frame] [dotted rule] [script] Letters of | EMILY DICKIN-SON | [leaf design] | EDITED BY MABEL LOOMIS TODD | WITH AN INTRODUCTION BY | MARK VAN DOREN | [two lines within a single-rule frame] *Cleveland* [publisher's logo] *New York* | THE WORLD PUBLISHING COMPANY

xxiv, 389 pp. Dust jacket. The copyright page reads *'First printing January* 1951' and 'HC1250'. Copyright, 22 January 1951. Deposit copy: DLC (9 April 1951). Inscribed copies: MA (January 1951), MAJ (16 January 1951). Price, $3.75. *Locations:* DLC, JM, MA, MAJ, MB, MH, NN, NNC, NcD, NcU, NjP, PSt, RPB, WU.

A 3.3.b
Third edition, first English printing (1951)

[seven lines within a single-rule frame] [dotted rule] [script] Letters of | EMILY DICKIN-SON | [leaf design] | EDITED BY MABEL LOOMIS TODD | WITH AN INTRODUCTION BY | MARK VAN DOREN | [three lines within a single-rule frame] LONDON | VICTOR GOLLANCZ LTD | 1951

Dust jacket. The copyright page reads "Copyright, 1951, by The World Publishing Company | PRINTED IN GREAT BRITAIN AT THE PITMAN PRESS, BATH'. Listed in the *English Catalogue* for 11 February 1952. Deposit copy: BL (25 January 1952). MAJ copy received 28 February 1952; MH copy (rebound) received 30 April 1952; DLC copy received 3 June 1952. Price, 21s. *Locations:* BL, CSt, CaMWU, CaNFSM, CaOLU, DLC, JM, MAJ, MH.

A 3.3.c
Third edition, second American printing [1962]

[all within a single-rule frame, surrounding an ornamental frame, both surrounding a single-rule frame] LETTERS OF | [script] Emily Dickinson | EDITED BY | MABEL LOO-MIS TODD | INTRODUCTION BY | MARK VAN DOREN | [publisher's logo] | [script] The Universal Library | GROSSET & DUNLAP | NEW YORK

Wrappers. *Grosset's Universal Library* UL144. The copyright page reads 'UNIVERSAL LIBRARY EDITION, 1962'. Price, $1.95. *Locations:* GTA, NjP, White.

A 4 POEMS: THIRD SERIES

A 4.1.a
Only edition, first printing (1896)

POEMS

BY

EMILY DICKINSON

Edited by

MABEL LOOMIS TODD

THIRD SERIES

BOSTON
ROBERTS BROTHERS
1896

A 4.1.a: 6^{13}/$_{16}$″ × 4^{3}/$_{8}$″

Copyright, 1896,

BY ROBERTS BROTHERS.

University Press:

JOHN WILSON AND SON, CAMBRIDGE, U. S. A.

[i–vii] viii [1] 2–9 [10–13] 14–70 [71–72] 73–97 [98–100] 101–136 [137–138] 139–200

[a]⁴ [1]⁸ 2–12⁸ 13⁴

Contents: p. i: 'POEMS | BY | EMILY DICKINSON | *THIRD SERIES*'; p. ii: advertisement for *Poems* and *Poems: Second Series;* p. iii: title page; p. iv: copyright page; p. v: eight lines of verse, beginning *'It's all I have to bring to-day,';* p. vi: blank; pp. vii–viii: 'PREFACE.', signed 'M.L.T. | AMHERST, *October,* 1896.'; pp. 1–9: contents; p. 10: blank; p. 11: 'I. | LIFE.'; p. 12: blank; pp. 13–70: poems; p. 71: 'II. | LOVE.'; p. 72: blank; pp. 73–97: poems; p. 98: blank; p. 99: 'III. | NATURE.'; p. 100: blank; pp. 101–136: poems; p. 137: 'IV. | TIME AND ETERNITY.'; p. 138: blank; pp. 139–200: poems.

Typography and paper: 3⅞″ (3⁹⁄₁₆″) × 3″; laid paper with horizontal chain marks 1³⁄₁₆″ apart; various lines per page. Running heads: rectos: pp. 3–9: *'CONTENTS.';* pp. 15–69, 73–97, 101–135, 139–199: *'POEMS.';* versos: p. viii: *'PREFACE.';* pp. 2–8: *'CONTENTS.';* pp. 14–70, 74–96, 102–136, 140–200: *'POEMS.'.*

Binding: Two styles have been noted, priority undetermined:

Binding A: Three-piece binding: medium yellow-green V cloth (smooth) spine, extending over to meet white V cloth (smooth) on front and back covers, the meeting of the two cloths marked by a goldstamped vertical straight rule; front cover: goldstamped '[ornate capitals] POEMS | [design] | [two lines in ornate printing] · Emily · Dickinson · | Third Series | [Indian pipes]'; back cover: blank; spine: goldstamped '[ornate capitals] POEMS | [two lines in ornate printing] Third | Series | [Indian pipes] | [two lines in ornate printing] Emily | Dickinson | BOSTON | ROBERTS BROS.'. Laid flyleaves; or no flyleaves. Laid or wove endpapers. All edges trimmed. All edges gilded. See *note two.*

Binding B: Medium gray or medium olive V cloth (smooth); bevelled edges; front cover: goldstamped '[ornate capitals] POEMS | [design] | [two lines in ornate printing] · Emily · Dickinson · | Third Series | [Indian pipes]'; back cover: blank; spine: goldstamped the same as in Binding A. Copies have been noted with 'LITTLE · BROWN | AND · COMPANY.' goldstamped at the base of the spine (see *note four*). Laid or wove flyleaves. Front wove and back laid; or wove; or laid endpapers. All edges trimmed. Top edges gilded.

Publication: 1,000 copies printed 8 April 1896. Prices: Binding A, $1.50; Binding B, $1.25.

On 31 December 1895, Mrs. Todd wrote E. D. Hardy of Roberts Brothers that she was sending him the manuscript for *Poems: Third Series* (MA). Hardy wrote Mrs. Todd on 7 January 1896 that the manuscript had gone "to the printer," and she wrote in her diary on 15 January 1896, "Proof of E. D., Third Series" arrived (MA; CtY). On 19 February 1896, she wrote in her diary, "I wrote *Preface* to E. D. Third Series, and sent off proof, plates, and Contents proof" (CtY). And on 22 March 1896, Mrs. Todd wrote Hardy that the "plate proofs . . . came today" (MA).

Noted for 1 September 1896 in *Publishers' Weekly* 50 (29 August 1896), 272. Listed in *Publishers' Weekly* 50 (12 September 1896), 334. Deposited for copyright: title, 7 February 1896; book, 6 May 1896. Copyright registration A9027. Deposit copy: Binding B: DLC (6 May 1896). Inscribed copies: Binding A: NN (from Lavinia Dickinson, 25 December 1896); Binding B: MB (from T. W. Higginson, 1 March 1896), JM (from Lavinia Dickinson, September 1896), ViU (October 1896), NcU (1 December 1896), NNC (from Lavinia Dickinson, 25 December 1896). MBAt copy (Binding B) received 9 September 1896. MB copy (rebound) received 23 September 1896. Royalty, 10% on all copies sold.

Printing: Electrotyped by John Wilson and Son. For printer's imprint, see copyright page illustration.

Locations: Binding A: IEN, InU, MA, NN, NNC, NjP, ViU; Binding B: CSt, CtY, DLC, FU, ICN, JM, MA, MAJ, MB, MBAt, MH, NN, NNC, NcU, NjP, RPB, ViU, WU.

Note one: A white silk ribbon marker is present in some copies.

Note two: Copies of *Poems: Third Series* in the three-piece bindings (Binding A) have had the page edges trimmed more than have those copies in the single casings (Binding B); the page size is usually ⅛" smaller.

Note three: Nearly all the copies of all the printings of *Poems: Third Series* contain mixed gatherings on thin and thick laid paper; for further information, see William White, "Emily Dickinson's 'Poems: Third Series': A Bibliographical Note," and Josiah Q. Bennett, "A Footnote to Mr. White's Article on *Poems: Third Series*," *Serif* 9 no. 2 (Summer 1972), 37–41, 41–42.

Note four: The copies with the Little, Brown imprint goldstamped at the base of the spine (CtY, NjP) were bound after June 1898, when Roberts Brothers was purchased by Little, Brown, and Company.

A 4.1.b
Second printing (1896)

Boston: Roberts Brothers, 1896.

The copyright page reads 'SECOND EDITION.'. Three-piece (medium yellow-green shelfback with white covers) bindings, or medium gray or medium olive (with bevelled edges) casings, with either Roberts Brothers or Little, Brown imprint goldstamped at the base of the spine—all V cloth (smooth). A white silk ribbon marker is present in some copies. 1,000 copies printed 21 September 1896. Inscribed copy: NjP (25 December 1896). *Locations:* CtY, JM, MA, MAJ, NN, NjP, RPB, ViU, WU.

Note: Copies with the Little, Brown imprint goldstamped at the base of the spine (CtY, NjP, WU) were bound after June 1898, when Roberts Brothers was purchased by Little, Brown, and Company.

A 4.1.c
Third printing (1906)

Boston: Little, Brown, and Company, 1906.

'SECOND EDITION.'. The same contents as in A 4.1.a, except: p. ii: blank. Medium gray V cloth (smooth) with front and back covers blank and goldstamping on the spine or with goldstamping on the front cover and the spine. *Locations:* MAJ, White.

A 4.1.d
Fourth printing (1911)

Boston: Little, Brown, and Company, 1911.

'SECOND EDITION.'. Light gray V cloth (smooth) with front and back covers blank and goldstamping on the spine. *Locations:* MA, NjP, PSt, WU, White.

A 4.1.e
Fifth printing (1914)

Boston: Little, Brown, and Company, 1914.

No "edition" designation appears on the copyright page of this and subsequent Little, Brown reprintings. Calendered paper. Light or medium gray V cloth (smooth) with front and back covers blank and goldstamping on the spine. Dust jacket of unprinted light yellow-brown paper. *Locations:* CtY (dust jacket), MAJ.

Note one: The following variant between the fourth and fifth printings is present:

iv.3–4   [gothic] University Press: | JOHN WILSON AND SON, CAMBRIDGE, U.S.A.
[[gothic] Printers | S. J. PARKHILL & CO., BOSTON, U.S.A.

Note two: A copy has been noted composed of gatherings 1–12 of the fifth printing and gathering 13 of the sixth printing, apparently a binding oddity suggesting that copies of the sheets of the fifth printing may have been bound up as needed through at least 1917: NjP.

A 4.1.f
Sixth printing (1917)

Boston: Little, Brown, and Company, 1917.

Wove paper. Light gray or light olive-gray V cloth (smooth) with front and back covers blank and goldstamping or greenstamping on the spine. *Locations:* IEN, MA, NjP, RPB, WU.

A 4.1.g
Seventh printing (1922)

Boston: Little, Brown, and Company, 1922.

Collation: $[1-6^{16} 7^8]$. Signed $[1]^{12}$ $2-8^8$ $[9]^8$ $10-12^8$ 13^4. Light olive-gray V cloth (smooth) with front and back covers blank and goldstamping or greenstamping on the spine. *Locations:* MA, MAJ, MH, NN, NcU, NjP, WU.

Note one: The following variant between the sixth and seventh printings is present:

iv.3–4   [*printer's imprint*] [[*not present*]

Note two: Klaus Lubbers estimates the total sales of *Poems: Third Series* at 3,500 copies (*Emily Dickinson: The Critical Revolution* [Ann Arbor: University of Michigan Press, 1968], p. 241).

A 4.1.h
Eighth printing (1967)

Gainesville, Fla.: Scholars' Facsimiles & Reprints, 1967.

Facsimile reprinting of A 4.1.a, combined with *Poems* (A 1.1.a) and *Poems: Second Series* (A 2.1.a) in three-volumes-in-one format; see A 1.1.ii for further information.

A5 THE SINGLE HOUND

A5.1.a
Only edition, first printing (1914)

THE SINGLE HOUND

POEMS OF A LIFETIME

BY

EMILY DICKINSON

WITH AN INTRODUCTION BY HER NIECE
MARTHA DICKINSON BIANCHI

BOSTON
LITTLE, BROWN, AND COMPANY
1914

A 5.1.a: 7$\frac{11}{16}$″ × 5$\frac{1}{16}$″

[i–v] vi–xix [xx–xxi] xxii–xxvi [1–3] 4–151 [152–154]

[1–11⁸ 12²]

Contents: p. i: 'THE SINGLE HOUND'; p. ii: blank; p. iii: title page; p. iv: copyright page; p. v–xix: 'THE EDITOR'S PREFACE.', signed 'MARTHA DICKINSON | BIANCHI.'; p. xx: blank: pp. xxi–xxvi: contents; p. 1: '*TO SUE.* | [16 lines of verse]'; p. 2: '[eight lines of verse] | — *Emilie.*'; pp. 3–151: poems; pp. 152–154: blank.

Typography and paper: 4³⁄₁₆″ (3¹⁵⁄₁₆″) × 3″; wove paper, watermarked 'OLDE STYLE'; 24 lines per page; various lines per page for poetry. Running heads: rectos: pp. vii–xix: '*PREFACE.*'; pp. xxiii–xxv: '*CONTENTS.*'; pp. 1–151: '*THE SINGLE HOUND.*'; versos: pp. vi–xviii: '*PREFACE.*'; pp. xxii–xxvi: '*CONTENTS.*'; p. 2: '*TO SUE.*'; pp. 4–150: '*THE SINGLE HOUND.*'.

Binding: White V cloth (smooth) spine, extending over to meet white paper-covered boards on the front and back covers; front and back covers: blank; spine: four raised bands with 'THE | SINGLE | HOUND | [rule] | EMILY | DICKINSON' between the first and second bands. Wove endpapers. Top edges trimmed, front and bottom edges rough-trimmed.

Dust jacket: Two styles have been noted, priority undetermined:

Style A: Unprinted glassine.

Style B: Unprinted glassine with spiderweb pattern.

Box: White calendered paper-covered box open at one end, with paper label on spine: '[rule] | [rule] | The | Single | Hound | [rule] | Emily | Dickinson | [rule] | [rule]'.

Publication: 595 copies printed 19 September 1914. The copyright page reads 'Published, September, 1914'. Advertised in *Publishers' Weekly* 86 (26 September 1914), 886. Listed in *Publishers' Weekly* 86 (3 October 1914), 1118. Copyright application received, 23 September 1914; books received, 23 September 1914. Copyright registration A 380532. Copyright renewed, 23 March 1942. According to the publisher's records, published 19 September 1914. Deposit copy: DLC (23 September 1914). Inscribed copies: NN (September 1914), IEN (5 October 1914). MB copy (rebound) received 22 September 1914; MBAt copy (rebound) received 30 September 1914. Price, $1.25.

Printing: Printed and bound by the University Press, Cambridge, Mass.

Locations: CSt, CtY (dust jacket A, box), DLC, FU, ICN, IEN, InU, JM, MA, MAJ (dust jacket B), MB, MH, NN, NNC, NcU, NjP, PSt, RPB, ViU, WU.

A 5.1.b
Second printing (1915)

Boston: Little, Brown, and Company, 1915.

293 copies printed 29 October 1915. Inscribed copies: NcD, PSt (both 25 December 1915). DLC copy (rebound) received 4 February 1916. *Locations:* CtY, IEN, InU, JM, MA, MAJ, NcD, NjP, PSt, RPB.

Note: The following variants between the first and second printings are present:

  iv.5   Published, September, 1914   [[*omitted*]
  iv.6   THE UNIVERSITY PRESS, CAMBRIDGE, U.S.A   [[gothic] Printers | S. J. PARKHILL & CO., BOSTON, U.S.A.

A 6 FURTHER POEMS OF EMILY DICKINSON

A 6.1.a
Only edition, first printing (1929)

FURTHER POEMS
OF EMILY DICKINSON

WITHHELD FROM PUBLICATION
BY HER SISTER LAVINIA

✦

EDITED BY HER NIECE
MARTHA DICKINSON BIANCHI
AND ALFRED LEETE HAMPSON

✦   ✦

✦   ✦

LITTLE, BROWN, AND COMPANY

BOSTON   ✦   ✦   1929

A 6.1.a: 7½″ × 5⅛″; the designs are in medium green

[i–v] vi–xx [1–2] 3–37 [38–40] 41–50 [51–52] 53–86 [87–88] 89–112 [113–114] 115–132 [133–134] 135–193 [194–195] 196–202 [203] 204–208

$[1–12^8 \ 13^{10} \ 14^8]$

Contents: p. i: 'FURTHER POEMS | OF EMILY DICKINSON'; p. ii: blank; p. iii: title page; p. iv: copyright page; pp. v–xx: 'INTRODUCTION', signed 'MARTHA DICKINSON BIANCHI | *July, 1928* | THE EVERGREENS, | AMHERST, MASSACHUSETTS'; p. 1: 'ONE'; p. 2: blank; pp. 3–37: poems; p. 38: blank; p. 39: 'TWO'; p. 40: blank; pp. 41–50: poems; p. 51: 'THREE'; p. 52: blank; pp. 53–86: poems; p. 87: 'FOUR'; p. 88: blank; pp. 89–112: poems; p. 113: 'FIVE'; p. 114: blank; pp. 115–132: poems; p. 133: 'SIX'; p. 134: blank; pp. 135–193: poems; p. 194: blank; pp. 195–202: 'APPENDIX'; pp. 203–208: 'INDEX OF FIRST LINES'.

Typography and paper: 5⅜″ × 3½″; laid paper with vertical chain marks ¹³⁄₁₆″ apart; 30 lines per page; various lines per page for poetry. No running heads.

Binding: Dark grayish green V cloth (smooth); front cover: goldstamped '[rule with three star-like designs forming a triangle in the center] | FURTHER POEMS | OF EMILY DICKINSON | [rule with three star-like designs forming a triangle in the center, with a vertical rule descending from the middle design]'; back cover: blank; spine: goldstamped '[star-like design] | FURTHER | POEMS | OF | EMILY | DICKINSON | [star-like design with a vertical rule descending from the bottom] | LITTLE, BROWN | AND COMPANY | [star-like design]'. Wove endpapers. All edges trimmed. Top edges gilded.

Dust jacket: Very light yellow-brown wove paper; front cover: green printing with purplish pink designs: '[rule with three star-like designs forming a triangle in the center] | FURTHER POEMS | OF EMILY DICKINSON | [rule with three star-like designs forming a triangle in the center] | WITHHELD FROM PUBLICATION BY | HER SISTER LAVINIA | [star-like design] | EDITED BY HER NIECE | MARTHA DICKINSON BIANCHI | AND ALFRED LEETE HAMPSON | [two star-like designs] | [10-line blurb for the book]'; back cover: blank; spine: green printing with purplish pink designs: '[star-like design] | FURTHER | POEMS | OF | EMILY | DICKINSON | [star-like design with a vertical rule descending from the bottom] | LITTLE, BROWN | AND COMPANY | [star-like design]'; front flap: advertisement and blurb for *Complete Poems;* back flap: blank.

Review copy: Unbound, sewn folded and gathered signatures (measuring 7¾″ × 5⅛″, untrimmed, with a two-leaf gathering of stiff wove paper at the front and back).

Publication: 2,000 copies printed 25 February 1929. The copyright page reads 'Published, March, 1929'. Advertised for 26 March 1929, in *Publishers' Weekly* 115 (9 March 1929), advertising section. Listed in *Publishers' Weekly* 115 (16 March 1929), 1418. Copyright application received, 9 March 1929; books received, 9 March 1929. Copyright registration A4800. Copyright renewed, 26 December 1956. According to

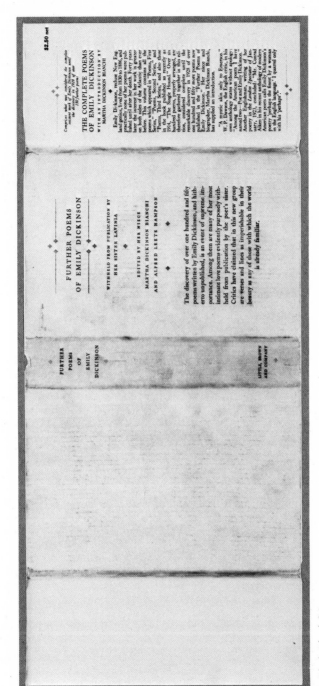

$2.50 net

THE COMPLETE POEMS
OF EMILY DICKINSON
WITH AN INTRODUCTION BY
MARTHA DICKINSON BIANCHI

Emily Dickinson, recluse New England genius, lived from 1830 to 1886, and practically none of her poems were published until after her death. Forty years later the interest in her work is greater on both sides of the Atlantic than ever before. This volume contains all the poems which appeared in "Poems, First Series," "Poems, Second Series," and "Poems, Third Series," and also those in the book published as recently as 1914, "The Single Hound." Over six hundred poems, properly arranged, are therefore gathered together in this edition, considered complete until the remarkable discovery in 1929 of over one hundred and fifty more poems now published in the "Further Poems of Emily Dickinson." Her niece and biographer, Martha Dickinson Bianchi, has supplied an introduction.

"A mystic akin only to Emerson," W. J. Dawson, the English critic, in his own anthology states without apology. "Among the American poets I have named two—Poe and Emily Dickinson." Another Englishman, writing of her poetry in the *London Spectator* of January, 1923, concluded, "Mr. Conrad Aiken in his recent anthology of modern American poets calls Emily Dickinson's poetry perhaps the finest by a woman in the English language." I quarrel only with his 'perhaps.'

FURTHER POEMS
OF EMILY DICKINSON

WITHHELD FROM PUBLICATION BY
HER SISTER LAVINIA

EDITED BY HER NIECE
MARTHA DICKINSON BIANCHI
AND ALFRED LEETE HAMPSON

The discovery of over one hundred and fifty poems written by Emily Dickinson, and hitherto unpublished, is an event of supreme importance. Among them are many of her most intimate love poems evidently purposely withheld from publication by the poet's sister. Critics have claimed that in this new group are verses and lines as imperishable in their beauty as any of those with which the world is already familiar.

FURTHER
POEMS
OF
EMILY
DICKINSON

LITTLE, BROWN
AND COMPANY

Dust jacket for A 6.1.a

Four hundred and sixty-five copies
of this Limited Edition
have been printed.
Of the four hundred and fifty copies
which are for sale
this is copy /*3*

Statement of limitation for A 6.1.b

the publisher's records, published 8 March 1929. Inscribed copy: MA (15 March 1929). MH copy received 19 March 1929; another MH copy received 23 March 1929; RPB copy received 28 March 1929. Price, $2.50.

Printing:　Composed by J. S. Cushing Company, Norwood, Mass.; printed and bound by Rockwell & Churchill Press, Boston.

Locations:　CtY (dust jacket), CtY (review copy), DLC, FU, IEN, InU (dust jacket), JM, MA (dust jacket), MAJ (dust jacket), MH (two copies) (dust jacket), NN (dust jacket), NjP (dust jacket), PSt, RPB, ScU, ViU (dust jacket), WU (dust jacket).

A 6.1.b
Second printing (1929)

Boston: Little, Brown, and Company, 1929. The title page is the same as in the first printing.

[i–iv]; pp. 1–208 are the same as in the first printing; [209–212]

[1–13⁸ 14⁶ 15⁸]

$[1-13^8 \ 14^6 \ 15^8]$

Contents:　pp. i–ii: blank; p. iii: 'FURTHER POEMS | OF EMILY DICKINSON'; p. iv: blank; inserted leaf with facsimile of manuscript poem printed on the verso; p. i: title page; p. ii: copyright page, the same as in the first printing; p. iii: statement of limitation; p. iv: blank; pp. v–208: the same as in the first printing; pp. 209–210: blank; p. 211: colophon; p. 212: blank.

Typography and paper:　The same as in the first printing except: the page size is $8^{13}/_{16}'' \times 5\frac{3}{4}''$; wove paper.

Binding:　Blackish green V cloth (smooth) spine, extending over to meet medium yellowish green fine linen cloth on front and back covers; front and back covers: blank; spine: light pink paper label with green printing: '[star-like design] | FURTHER | POEMS | OF | EMILY | DICKINSON | [star-like design]'. Wove endpapers. Top edges trimmed, front and bottom edges rough-trimmed. Top edges gilded.

Dust jacket:　Unprinted glassine.

Box:　Light green-gray paper-covered cardboard box (open at one end) with light pink paper label with green printing on spine: '[star-like design] | FURTHER | POEMS | OF | EMILY | DICKINSON | [star-like design] | *Limited* | *Edition* | No.　| [star-like design]'.

Publication:　Printed 16 March 1929. Limited to 465 numbered copies, plus 15 copies, marked A–O, not for sale. Advertised for 16 March 1929, in *Publishers' Weekly* 115 (9 March 1929), advertising section. MH copy received 1 April 1929. Price, $7.50.

> ❖   ❖   ❖
>
> This book is composed in **Caslon Number 337 series**, faithfully reproduced by the **Lanston Monotype Machine Company of Philadelphia, Pennsylvania,** from the Old Caslon Series cut in the year 1720, by **William Caslon, the first, of London.**
>
> The composition and plates are the work of the **J. S. Cushing Company of Norwood, Massachusetts** and the book was printed by the **Rockwell and Churchill Press, Boston, Massachusetts on Rag Book Paper** made by the **Reading Paper Mills, Reading, Penn-** sylvania.
>
> The cover is a half binding in cloth with **green linen finish sides and the book was bound by the Riverside Bindery, Cambridge, Massachusetts.**
>
> ❖   ❖   ❖

Colophon for A 6.1.b

Locations: CtY (dust jacket, box), DLC, IEN (box), InU (box), JM (box), MA (dust jacket, box), MAJ (dust jacket, box), MB (box), MH (box), NN, NNC (box), NcU.

Note: A green silk ribbon marker is present in all copies.

A 6.1.c
Third printing (1929)

Boston: Little, Brown, and Company, 1929.

2,000 copies printed 8 March 1929. The copyright page reads 'Reprinted March, 1929'. Deposit copy: DLC (9 March 1929). Inscribed copy: MH (March 1929). MBAt copy received 19 March 1929. *Locations:* DLC, JM, MA, MAJ, MBAt, MH, WU.

A 6.1.d
Fourth printing (1929)

Boston: Little, Brown, and Company, 1929.

2,000 copies printed 20 March 1929. The copyright page reads "Reprinted March, 1929 (twice)'. Inscribed copy: MH (from Mrs. Bianchi, May 1929). ICN copy received 6 May 1929. *Locations:* ICN, JM, MH, NjP, PSt, RPB, WU.

A 6.1.e
Fifth printing (1929)

Boston: Little, Brown, and Company, 1929.

2,000 copies printed 3 April 1929. The copyright page reads 'Reprinted March, 1929 (three times)'. NN copy (rebound) received from the publisher 11 April 1929. *Locations:* MA, MAJ, MH.

A 6.1.f
Sixth printing (1929)

Two issues have been noted:

A 6.1.f₁
First (American) issue (1929)

Boston: Little, Brown, and Company, 1929.

2,000 copies printed 10 April 1929. The copyright page reads 'Reprinted April, 1929'. *Locations:* JM, MA, MAJ, NNC, ViU.

FURTHER POEMS
of
EMILY DICKINSON

EDITED BY HER NIECE
MARTHA DICKINSON BIANCHI
AND ALFRED LEETE HAMPSON

LONDON
MARTIN SECKER
1929

A 6.1.f₂: 7⅜″ × 5″

The pagination is the same as in the first printing

$[1-12^8 \, _{(+12)} \, 13^{10} \, 14^8]$ The title leaf is a cancel

Contents: The same as in the first printing, except: p. iii: English title page; p. iv: English publisher's imprint.

Typography and paper: The same as in the first printing, except for the page size.

Binding: Dark green V cloth (smooth); front and back covers: blank; spine: white paper label with '[all within a light green ornamental frame] FURTHER | POEMS OF | EMILY | DICKINSON | [rule] | SECKER'. Wove endpapers. All edges trimmed. Top edges stained blue.

Dust jacket: Cream laid paper with green printing: front cover: '[all within a single-rule frame surrounding an ornamental frame] FURTHER POEMS | *of* | EMILY DICKINSON | LONDON | MARTIN SECKER | 1929'; back cover: blank; spine: '[rule] | [ornamental frame] | FURTHER | POEMS OF | EMILY | DICKINSON | [floral design] | 10/6 | NET | SECKER | [ornamental frame] | [rule]'; front flap: 16-line blurb for the book; back flap: eight-line blurb for *Complete Poems [Pocket Edition]*.

Publication: Listed in the *English Catalogue* for October 1929. Deposit copies: BL (31 October 1929), BO (28 November 1929). MAJ copy received 12 February 1930. Price, 10s. 6d.

Locations: BL, BO, CtY (dust jacket), MAJ (dust jacket), RPB.

Note: Even though this issue was published in October 1929, it does not have the textual readings of the June 1929 American printing (see A 6.1.g). It is therefore presumably an issue of the previous (April 1929) American printing.

A 6.1.g
Seventh printing (1929)

Boston: Little, Brown, and Company, 1929.

2,000 copies printed 10 July 1929. The copyright page reads 'Reprinted June, 1929'. *Locations:* CtY, JM, MAJ, MH, PSt, White.

Note: The following textual changes are present: p. 203: "I'm sorry for the Dead to-day"; p. 204: blank; pp. 205–210: 'INDEX OF FIRST LINES'; pp. 211–212: blank.

A 6.1.h
Eighth printing (1930)

Boston: Little, Brown, and Company, 1930.

500 copies printed 22 May 1930. *Not seen.*

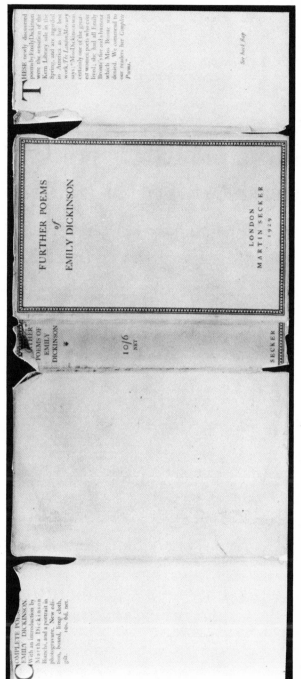

See back flap

THESE newly discovered poems by Emily Dickinson were the sensation of the Kern Library in the Spring, and are reprinted in America as fast as her work, *The London Mercury* says: "Mrs Dickinson was certainly one of the greatest women poets who ever lived; she had all Emily Brontë's fire and humour which Miss Brontë was denied. We commend to our readers her *Complete Poems*."

FURTHER POEMS

of

EMILY DICKINSON

LONDON
MARTIN SECKER
1929

FURTHER POEMS OF EMILY DICKINSON

10/6 NET

SECKER

COMPLETE POEMS OF EMILY DICKINSON. With an introduction by Martha Dickinson Bianchi, and a portrait in photogravure. New edition, boards, buckram cloth, gilt. 10s. 6d. net.

Dust jacket for A 6.1.f₂

A 7 UNPUBLISHED POEMS OF EMILY DICKINSON

A 7.1.a
Only edition, first printing (1935)

UNPUBLISHED POEMS

OF EMILY DICKINSON

**EDITED BY HER NIECE
MARTHA DICKINSON BIANCHI
AND ALFRED LEETE HAMPSON**

LITTLE, BROWN, AND COMPANY

BOSTON   **1935**

A 7.1.a: 8¾" × 3½"; the designs are in medium green

[i–viii] [1–2] 3–27 [28–30] 31–80 [81–82] 83–110 [111–112] 113–149 [150–153] 154–157 [158–160]

[1–10^8 11^4]   A frontispiece is inserted after leaf 1$_1$

Contents: p. i: 'UNPUBLISHED POEMS | OF EMILY DICKINSON'; p. ii: blank; inserted leaf with facsimile of manuscript poem printed on the verso; p. iii: title page; p. iv: copyright page; p. v: statement of limitation; p. vi: blank; p. vii: editor's note; p. viii: blank; p. 1: 'ONE'; p. 2: blank; pp. 3–27: poems; p. 28: blank; p. 29: 'TWO'; p. 30: blank; p. 31–80: poems; p. 81: 'THREE'; p. 82: blank; pp. 83–110: poems; p. 111: 'FOUR'; p. 112: blank; pp. 113–149: poems; p. 150: blank; p. 151: 'APPENDIX'; p. 152: blank; pp. 153–157: 'INDEX OF FIRST LINES'; pp. 158–160: blank.

Typography and paper: 5⅝" × 3½"; wove paper; 31 lines per page; various lines per page for poetry. No running heads.

Binding: Blackish green V cloth (smooth) spine, extending over to meet medium yellowish green fine linen cloth (B-like) on front and back covers; front and back covers: blank; spine: light pink paper label with green printing: '[star-like design] | UNPUBLISHED | POEMS | OF | EMILY | DICKINSON | [star-like design]'. Wove end-papers. Top edges trimmed, front and bottom edges rough-trimmed. Top edges gilded.

Dust jacket: Unprinted glassine.

Box: Grayish white paper-covered cardboard box (open at one end) with light pink paper label with green printing on the spine: '[star-like design] | UNPUBLISHED | POEMS | OF | EMILY | DICKINSON | [star-like design] | *Limited Edition* | No. | [star-like design]'.

Review copy: Sewn, trimmed sheets (measuring 8⁷⁄₁₆" × 5⅝"), bound in unprinted medium blue stiff paper wrappers, with leaf 1$_3$ (containing the statement of limitation) cancelled and with double wove front and back endpapers.

Publication: Limited to 525 numbered copies. The copyright page reads 'Published November, 1935'. Listed in *Publishers' Weekly* 128 (23 November 1935), 1910. Copyright application received, 23 November 1935; books received, 23 November 1935. Copyright registration A88356. Copyright renewed, 31 May 1963. According to the publisher's records, published 22 November 1935. Deposit copies: DLC (23 November 1935), two copies. Inscribed copies: ICN (19 November 1935), ViU (25 November 1935). NN copy received from the publisher 15 November 1935; MAJ copy received 21 November 1935; NcD copy received 25 November 1935; MBAt copy received 26 November 1935. Price, $7.50.

> *This edition consists of*
> *five hundred twenty-five numbered copies*
> *of which five hundred are offered for sale.*
>
> *This is copy* /35

Statement of limitation for A 7.1.a

Printing: Composed by J. S. Churchill, Norwood, Mass.; printed and bound by Rockwell & Churchill Press, Boston.

Locations: CSt (box), CtY (review copy), DLC (box), ICN, IEN, InU, JM (dust jacket, box), MA (dust jacket, box), MAJ (dust jacket, box), MB, MBAt, MH (box), NN (dust jacket, box), NNC (box), NcD, NjP (dust jacket, box), NjP (review copy), PSt (box), RPB, ViU (box), ViU (review copy), WU (box).

Note: A green silk ribbon marker is present in all copies except review copies.

A 7.1.b
Second printing (1936)

Boston: Little, Brown, and Company, 1936.

The pagination is the same as in the first printing

[1–9⁸ 10⁴ 11⁸]

Contents: pp. i–ii: blank; p. iii: 'UNPUBLISHED POEMS | OF EMILY DICKINSON'; p. iv: advertisement for three books by Dickinson and two on Dickinson by Martha Dickinson Bianchi; p. v: title page, the same as in the first printing, except: '1936' is substituted for '1935'; p. vi: copyright page, the same as in the first printing, except: new publication date (see below); pp. vii–160: the same as in the first printing.

Typography and paper: The same as in the first printing, except: the page size is 7½″ × 5⅛″.

Binding: Dark grayish green V cloth (smooth); front cover: goldstamped '[rule with three star-like designs forming a triangle in the center] | UNPUBLISHED POEMS | OF EMILY DICKINSON | [rule with three star-like designs forming a triangle in the center, with a vertical rule descending from the middle design]'; back cover: blank; spine: goldstamped '[star-like design] | UNPUBLISHED | POEMS | OF | EMILY | DICKINSON | [star-like design with a vertical rule descending from the bottom] | LITTLE, BROWN | AND COMPANY | [star-like design]'. Wove endpapers. All edges trimmed. Top edges gilded.

Dust jacket: White glossy paper; front cover: all within a green single-rule frame with a star-like design in each corner: 'UNPUBLISHED POEMS | OF EMILY DICKINSON | [green] *Edited by her Niece* | MARTHA DICKINSON BIANCHI | *and* ALFRED LEETE HAMPSON | [color photograph of white gardenia on black background] | [five-line blurb for the book] | — Percy Hutchison, *N. Y. Times Book Review*'; back cover: blank; spine: the same as the spine on the binding; front flap: 42-line blurb for *Unpublished Poems;* back flap: 39-line blurb for the Centenary Edition of *Poems.*

Publication: The copyright page reads 'Published February, 1936'. Advertised for 7 February 1936 in *Publishers' Weekly* 129 (25 January 1936), advertising section. Listed in *Publishers' Weekly* 129 (8 February 1936), 737. MB copy received 28 January 1936;

The Poems of
EMILY DICKINSON
Centenary Edition

WITH AN INTRODUCTION BY
MARTHA DICKINSON BIANCHI

Emily Dickinson, recluse New England genius, lived from 1830 to 1886, and practically none of her poems were published until 1890, four years after her death. Now the interest in her work is greater on both sides of the Atlantic than ever before. This volume contains all the poems which appeared in "Poems, First Series", "Poems, Second Series", and "Poems, Third Series", and also those in the book published in 1914, "The Single Hound", and the seven hundred and more poems discovered in 1928 and published in 1929, as the "Further Poems of Emily Dickinson". Her niece and biographer, Martha Dickinson Bianchi, has supplied an introduction.

"Mr. Conrad Aiken in his recent anthology of modern American poets calls Emily Dickinson's poetry 'perhaps the most . . . by a woman in the English language.' I quarrel only with his perhaps." —*Louise Spataro*. "Some of the greatest poems written since Sappho . . . magnificent as literature. The more I read them the more uncertain is my enthusiasm . . . Emily Dickinson's *Last Poems* is . . . she has become ever forty years after her death, inevitably the greatest woman poet in our language." —*John Gould Fletcher in his Lowell Review . . . of Literature*. "Emily Dickinson finds her place beside Poe and Whitman as a chief figure in the literature of those States. —*Isidore Dautal*.

UNPUBLISHED POEMS
OF EMILY DICKINSON

Edited for the First . . . by

MARTHA DICKINSON BIANCHI
and ALFRED LEETE HAMPSON

Whether or not we have had all the extant poetry of Emily Dickinson makes no difference. Nothing more that might follow could either add to her poetic stature or detract. This book is but further proof that she is of the immortals.
— *Percy Hutchinson, N. Y. Times Book Review*

UNPUBLISHED
POEMS
OF
EMILY
DICKINSON

LITTLE, BROWN
AND COMPANY

UNPUBLISHED POEMS
OF EMILY DICKINSON
EDITED BY
MARTHA DICKINSON BIANCHI
and ALFRED LEETE HAMPSON

In presenting these heretofore unpublished poems of Emily Dickinson nearly a half century after her death, Martha Dickinson Bianchi, niece and literary executor of the famous New England poet, makes the following statement:

"The preparation of *Emily Dickinson Face to Face*, published in 1932, led to an even more exhaustive examination of the accumulation of Dickinson family papers than I had ever made before. I also made a minute examination of the collection of Emily Dickinson manuscripts which I had supposed to contain nothing of value beyond the poems included in the first three volumes edited and published in 1890, 1891 and 1896, long before I inherited the manuscripts from my Aunt Lavinia. The work of deciphering, copying, and cataloguing the poems, and then checking them with the eight hundred or so poems included in the Centenary Edition was enormous—occupying a large portion of my time for more than three summers. I discovered the existence of various unpublished poems, which had been omitted by early editors in the nineties, and which had now been revealed during this prolonged and painstaking research.

"Many of the poems in this collection are unquestionably the equal of Emily Dickinson's best work although this is not true of all. Distinct from the unpublished mass of variants, comparatively experiments, trifling whimsies and unperfected fragments—the evident discard of the author—the one hundred and thirty-one poems here presented have emerged."

Dust jacket for A 7.1.b

MAJ copy received 6 February 1936; NN copy received from the publisher 8 February 1936. Price, $2.50.

Locations: CtY (dust jacket), IEN (dust jacket), InU (dust jacket), JM (dust jacket), MA (dust jacket), MAJ (dust jacket), MB, MH, NN, NNC, NcU, NjP (dust jacket), PSt, ViU (dust jacket), WU (dust jacket).

A 7.1.c
Third printing (1936)

Boston: Little, Brown, and Company, 1936.

The copyright page reads 'Reprinted February, 1936'. NjP copy received 14 April 1936. *Locations:* ICN, JM, NcU, NjP.

A 8 BOLTS OF MELODY

A 8.1.a
Only edition, first printing (1945)

BOLTS OF MELODY

NEW POEMS OF

EMILY DICKINSON

EDITED BY

MABEL LOOMIS TODD

AND

MILLICENT TODD BINGHAM

NEW YORK AND LONDON

HARPER & BROTHERS PUBLISHERS

1 9 4 5

A 8.1.a: 8⁷⁄₁₆″ × 5¼″; Dickinson's name, the design, and the date are in medium red

This book is complete and unabridged
in contents, and is manufactured in strict
conformity with Government regulations
for saving paper.

BOLTS OF MELODY

4 · 5

FIRST EDITION

C · U

[i–iv] v–xii [xiii–xiv] xv [xvi–xxi] xxii–xxix [xxx–xxxii] [1–2] 3–7 [8–10] 11–30 [31–32] 33–42 [43–44] 45–55 [56–58] 59–80 [81–82] 83–95 [96–98] 99–125 [126–128] 129–136 [137–138] 139–179 [180–182] 183–223 [224–226] 227–238 [239–240] 241–262 [263–264] 265–294 [295–296] 297–298 [299–300] 301–310 [311–312] 313 [314–316] 317–319 [320–322] 323–332 [333–336] 337–352

[1–12^6]

Contents: p. i: 'BOLTS OF MELODY | NEW POEMS OF | *EMILY DICKINSON* | [ornate rule]'; p. ii: advertisement for Mrs. Bingham's *Ancestors' Brocades* and her edition of the *Letters* (1931); p. iii: title page; p. iv: copyright page; pp. v–vi: 'FOREWORD', signed 'Mark Van Doren | *Falls Village, Connecticut* | 20 *October* 1944'; pp. vii–xxviii: 'INTRODUCTION', signed 'M. T. B. | *Washington, D.C.* | 20 *October* 1944' [facsimiles of manuscript poems on pp. xiii–xiv and xvi–xxi]; p. xxix: contents; p. xxx: blank; p. xxxi: 24 lines of verse, beginning '*I would not paint a picture*'; p. xxxii: blank; p. 1: 'PART ONE'; p. 2: blank; pp. 3–7: introduction to Part One; p. 8: blank; p. 9: '*The Far Theatricals of Day*'; p. 10; blank; pp. 11–30: poems; p. 31: '*The Round Year*'; p. 32: blank; pp. 33–42: poems; p. 43: '*My Pageantry*'; p. 44: blank; pp. 45–55: poems; p. 56: blank; p. 57: *Our Little Kinsmen*'; p. 58: blank; pp. 59–80: poems; p. 81: '*Once a Child*'; p. 82: blank; pp. 83–95: poems; p. 96: blank; p. 97: '*The Mob within the Heart*'; p. 98: blank; pp. 99–125: poems; p. 126: blank; p. 127: '*Italic Faces*'; p. 128: blank; pp. 129–136: poems; p. 137: '*The Infinite Aurora*'; p. 138: blank; pp. 139–179: poems; p. 180: blank; p. 181: '*The White Exploit*'; pp. 182–223: poems; p. 224: blank; p. 225: '*Vital Light*'; p. 226: blank; pp. 227–238: poems; p. 239: '*That Campaign Inscrutable*'; p. 240: blank; pp. 241–262: poems; p. 263: '*An Ablative Estate*'; p. 264: blank; pp. 265–294: poems; p. 295: 'PART TWO'; p. 296: blank; pp. 297–298: introduction to Part Two; p. 299: '*Poems Incomplete or Unfinished*'; p. 300: blank; pp. 301–310: poems; pp. 311–312: facsimiles of manuscript poems; p. 313: poem; p. 314: blank; p. 315: '*Fragments*'; p. 316: blank; pp. 317–319: poems; p. 320: blank; p. 321: '*Poems Personal and Occasional*'; p. 322: blank; pp. 323–333: poems; p. 334: blank; p. 335: 'INDEX OF FIRST LINES'; p. 336: blank; pp. 337–352: index of first lines.

Typography and paper: 6¾" (6½") × 4"; wove paper; 38 lines per page; various lines per page for poetry. Running heads: rectos: pp. ix–xi, xv, xxiii–xxvii: 'Introduction'; pp.

5–7: 'Part One'; pp. 13–29, 35–41, 47–55, 61–79, 85–95, 101–125, 131–135, 141–179, 185–195, 199–201, 205–207, 211–213, 217–223, 229–237, 243–261, 267–293, 303–309, 313, 319, 325–331: titles of sections; pp. 339–351: 'Index of First Lines'; versos: pp. vi, viii–xii, xxii–xxviii, 4–6, 12–30, 34–42, 46–54, 60–80, 84–94, 100–124, 130–136, 140–178, 184–190, 194–222, 228–238, 242–262, 266–294, 298, 302–310, 318, 324–332, 338–352: 'BOLTS OF MELODY'.

Binding: Dark yellowish green V cloth (smooth); front cover: blindstamped rectangular publisher's logo in bottom right corner; back cover: blank; spine: goldstamped 'Bolts of | Melody | [rule] | *New Poems* | *of* | Emily Dickinson | [rule] | TODD | AND | BINGHAM | HARPER'. Wove endpapers. All edges trimmed.

Dust jacket: White or white glossy paper; front cover: '[two lines in white on dark red background] OVER 650 HITHERTO UNPUBLISHED | POEMS BY EMILY DICKINSON | [white uneven rule] | [pale greenish blue uneven rule] | [white uneven rule] | [dark red uneven rule] | [white uneven rule] | [pale greenish blue uneven rule] | [white uneven rule] | [dark red uneven rule] | [white uneven rule] | [four lines on pale greenish blue background] [two lines in white script] Bolts of [with, from top to bottom, 'WONG' at right] | Melody | [two lines in dark red] NEW POEMS OF | EMILY DICKINSON | [white uneven rule] | [dark red uneven rule] | [white uneven rule] | [pale greenish blue uneven rule] | [white uneven rule] | [dark red uneven rule] | [white uneven rule] | [pale greenish blue uneven rule] | [white uneven rule] | [three lines on dark red background] [two lines in white] EDITED BY MABEL LOOMIS TODD | AND MILLICENT TODD BINGHAM | [dark greenish blue script] Harper and Brothers Established 1817'; back cover: blurbs for the book, in dark red printing on white background, by Mark Van Doren and George Whicher; spine: '[dark red block] | [white uneven rule] | [pale greenish blue uneven rule] | [white uneven rule] | [dark red uneven rule] | [white uneven rule] | [pale greenish blue uneven rule] | [white uneven rule] | [dark red uneven rule] | [white uneven rule] | [five lines on pale greenish blue background] [two lines in dark red script] Bolts of | Melody | [group of six flowers and stems in white] | [two lines in dark red] EMILY | DICKINSON | [white uneven rule] | [dark red uneven rule] | [white uneven rule] | [pale greenish blue uneven rule] | [white uneven rule] | [dark red uneven rule] | [white uneven rule] | [pale greenish blue uneven rule] | [white uneven rule] | [dark red uneven rule] | [white script] Harper'; front and back flaps: description of the book in dark red printing on white background.

Publication: The publisher's code ('C-U') indicates May 1945 printing. Published 4 April 1945, according to *Publishers' Weekly* 147 (7 April 1945), 1498. Copyright application received, 6 April 1945; books received, 23 March 1945. Copyright registration A187679. Copyright renewed, 3 April 1973. According to the publisher's records, published 4 April 1945. Deposit copies: DLC (23 March 1945), two copies. Inscribed copies: ICN (5 April 1945), RPB (from Mrs. Bingham, 22 April 1945). MAJ copy received 30 March 1945; MA copy received 2 April 1945; MH copy received 4 April 1945; MAJ copy received 5 April 1945. Price, $3.00.

Printing: Printed and bound by the Haddon Craftsmen, Haddon, Pa.

Locations: CtY (dust jacket), DLC (dust jacket), FU, ICN, IEN (dust jacket), InU, JM (dust jacket), MA (dust jacket), MAJ (two copies) (dust jacket), MB (dust jacket), MBAt, MH, NNC (dust jacket), NcU, NjP (dust jacket), PSt (dust jacket), RPB (dust jacket), ScU, ViU, WU (dust jacket).

Note one: A set of partial galley proofs has been noted: CtY.

Note two: A salesman's dummy has been noted: black stiff paper covers: front cover recto: silverstamped at left, from bottom to top: 'Harper & Brothers *Publishers* New York N.Y. | [rule] | [rule]' and in the center: all within a silverstamped double-rule frame:

BOLTS OF MELODY

New Poems of Emily Dickinson

Edited by MABEL LOOMIS TODD
and MILLICENT TODD BINGHAM

There can be no doubt that the appearance of this volume of hitherto unpublished poems by Emily Dickinson is a literary event of first importance. To say how would be understatement.

The history of this remarkable book goes back to stage when, following the publication of *Poems, Third Series*, Mabel Loomis Todd's painstaking work on the poems came to an abrupt end. The story surrounding it—an undetermate episode lost in the obscurity of nearly fifty years—has been told in *Ancestors' Brocades*, by Mrs. Todd's daughter. It was upon the request of her mother, Millicent Todd Bingham, undertook the complicated work of continuing the poems of Emily Dickinson. There were hundreds of these, over half had never been published. Many had been neatly copied in ink and tied into small bundles by the author; others, also in clear copy, were in numbered envelopes. The rest that remained were scribbled in pencil on scraps of paper, on the backs of old envelopes and letters. These were often torn across so that words and often whole lines of words on the division into lines and stanzas was left to the discretion of the latter. The challenge to the editor was

(continued on last flap)

(Continued from front flap)

remarkable. Mrs. Bingham has answered that challenge, giving years of exhausting devotion, patience and judgment to the task of copying, sorting, and correcting errors in transcription in order to present to the public this volume of over six hundred and fifty unpublished poems, many of which represent the poet's finest work, written in her fullest maturity.

The arrangement of the poems is of unusual interest, revealing the entire range of Emily Dickinson's scope of the poet's insight. The book falls naturally into two parts. The first leads from the world without, the aspects of nature, into the revelation of human nature, of the apprehensions from childhood to the mystery of death. It culminates in their group of philosophical poems on the significance of life, many of which were written in Emily Dickinson's last years. The second part is devoted to occasional and personal poems, bits of verse sent with gifts and fragments that are brilliant in themselves. Mrs. Bingham has presented a chronology of expression both thoughtful and dramatic.

The resulting volume is a gift of inestimable value to the large audience which has long recognized the genius of Emily Dickinson. Although her personal life was devoted to memory, the greatness of her work acclaimed all over the world, is as fresh and exciting today as it was sixty years ago.

Mark Van Doren has written a foreword to the book.

B-3420

Mark Van Doren writes in his foreword to *Bolts of Melody*—

"... Mrs. Bingham's book is news of that mysterious person and that great poet, and it is news on so impressive a scale that one may well hesitate to improvise a statement of its value. The value of a fine poem—and many here are among Emily Dickinson's finest, even after years during which it might have been supposed that all the best were out—is scarcely to be stated anyhow. Such a poem states itself, as these immediately tell to scholar, to poet, and to layman in America who understand that Emily Dickinson is great not merely in their country but everywhere.

"The task of editing her, as scholar at least are sure to know, is both a tease and a torture. . . . It has been my privilege to watch Mrs. Bingham at work upon these poems, and it is my pleasure to say how much I admire the quality no less than the quaintity of her devotion. Her mother, Mrs. Todd, was Emily Dickinson's first editor. She was superb in the role, and Mrs. Bingham has everywhere been faithful to the challenge she inherited."

George Whicher, author of This Was a Poet: A Critical Biography of Emily Dickinson, *says of* Bolts of Melody:

"*Bolts of Melody* is well named. The production of 668 new poems by Emily Dickinson, including some of her maturest and best lines, is the most stunning surprise in the history of American literature. It is an asked joy, and one to which we have long been unaccustomed, that the difficult work of transcribing and editing the manuscripts has been performed with a tact and intelligence that are beyond cavil."

OVER 650 HITHERTO UNPUBLISHED
POEMS BY EMILY DICKINSON

Bolts of Melody

NEW POEMS OF

EMILY DICKINSON

EDITED BY MABEL LOOMIS TODD
AND MILLICENT TODD BINGHAM

Harper

Harper and Brothers Established 1817

Bolts of Melody EMILY DICKINSON

Dust jacket for A 8.1.a

reddish orange paper label with '[all within a single-rule frame] Bolts of Melody | [rule] | MABEL LOOMIS TODD | MILLICENT TODD BINGHAM'; front cover verso and back cover recto and verso: blank. Inside is a two-leaf gathering of stiff gray paper: p. [1]: stapled on it is a gathering of [1]^8: p. [a]: title page, with Dickinson's name, the design, and the date in light green; p. [b]: printed blank for size of book, probable price, and probable publication date; pp. [c–d]: 'SYNOPSIS'; p. [e]: contents; p. [f]: blank; pp. [g–h]: 'FOREWORD', dated *'October ??, 1944'*; p. [i]: *'I would not paint a picture'*; p. 25: poems 48, 110; p. 26: poems 110 (continued), 147, 233; p. 27: poems 239, 620, 644, 645; p. 28: poem 647; pp. [n–p]: blank, with leaf 1$_8$ pasted to gray cardboard backing; p. [2]: blank; p. [3]: front cover of dust jacket; p. [4]: blank. *Location:* CtY.

A 8.1.b
Second printing (1945)

New York and London: Harper & Brothers, 1945.

Dickinson's name, the design, and the date are in red. The copyright page reads 'SECOND EDITION | D-U', indicating April 1945 printing. Inscribed copy: NjP (September 1945). *Locations:* ICN, MA, MH, NcD, NjP, RPB, WU.

A 8.1.c
Third printing (1945)

New York and London: Harper & Brothers, 1945.

Dickinson's name, the design, and the date are in red. The copyright page reads 'THIRD EDITION | E-U', indicating May 1945 printing. *Locations:* CtY, JM, MA, MAJ, NcD, RPB, WU.

A 8.1.d
Fourth printing [1946]

New York and London: Harper & Brothers, 1945 [i.e., 1946].

The title page is all in black, as are all subsequent reprintings. The copyright page reads 'L-V', indicating November 1946 printing. *Locations:* BL, CtY, InU, Lowenberg.

Note: The following textual variants between the third and fourth printings are present:

5.14–15	Love first and last of all things made | Of which our living world is but the shade. [Love is the fellow of the resurrection | Scooping up the dust and chanting "Live!"
125.6–14	[*Poem 232*] [[*poem omitted*]
317.17–19	[*Poem 627*] [[*poem omitted*]

A 8.1.e
Fifth printing for English sale [1946]

BOLTS OF MELODY

NEW POEMS OF

EMILY DICKINSON

EDITED BY

MABEL LOOMIS TODD

AND

MILLICENT TODD BINGHAM

JONATHAN CAPE
THIRTY BEDFORD SQUARE
LONDON

A 8.1.e: 8⅜″ × 5¼″

Pagination, collation, and typography and paper are the same as in the first printing.

Contents: The same as in the first printing, except: p. iii: English title page.

Binding: Medium bluish green V cloth (smooth); front and back covers: blank; spine: goldstamped 'BOLTS | OF | MELODY | [ornate rule] | EMILY | DICKINSON | [publisher's logo]'. Wove endpapers. All edges trimmed. Top edges stained light green.

Dust jacket: Cream wove paper; front cover: '[two lines in medium bluish green] BOLTS OF | MELODY | [black, medium bluish green, and light yellow abstract drawing by N. I. Cannon] | EMILY DICKINSON'; back cover: blank; spine: 'BOLTS | OF | MELODY | [medium bluish green triple rule] | EMILY | DICKINSON | [drawing, in the same colors, similar to the one on the front cover] | [medium bluish green publisher's logo]'; front flap: 30-line blurb for the book; back flap: blank.

Publication: The copyright page reads 'L-V', indicating November 1946 printing. Deposit copies: BL (2 September 1947), BO (9 September 1947). Price, 16s.

Printing: Manufactured by the Haddon Craftsmen, Haddon, Pa.

Locations: BL, BO, CaOTY, MH, NjP (dust jacket), RPB.

A 8.1.f
Sixth printing [1950]

New York and London: Harper and Brothers, [1950].

The copyright page reads 'C-Z', indicating March 1950 printing.

Location: MB

A 8.1.g
Seventh printing [1952]

New York: Harper and Brothers, [1952].

The copyright page reads 'H-B', indicating August 1952 printing.

Locations: MAJ, ViU.

A 8.1.h
Eighth printing [1955]

New York: Harper and Brothers, [1955].

The copyright page reads 'E-E', indicating May 1955 printing.

Location: NcD.

BOLTS OF MELODY

Edited by MABEL LOOMIS TODD and MILLICENT TODD BINGHAM

The publication here of over 650 new poems by Emily Dickinson is a noteworthy literary event. The remarkable story of their re-discovery and the work entailed in editing them is told by Mrs. Bingham in the Introduction.

The arrangement of the book reveals the variety of the subjects and the scope of the poet's insight. The first section leads from the world without, the aspects of nature, of the ages of man from childhood to the revelation of human nature, of the ages of man from childhood to the mystery of death. It culminates in three groups of philosophical poems, many of which were written in Emily Dickinson's last years. In the second section are found occasional and personal poems, and fragments that are brilliant in themselves.

The resulting volume is of inestimable value to the large audience which has long recognised the genius of Emily Dickinson. Although her personal life was shrouded in mystery, the greatness of her work has been acclaimed all over the world, and is as fresh and exciting today as it was sixty years ago.

16s. net

BOLTS
OF
MELODY

EMILY
DICKINSON

BOLTS OF MELODY

EMILY DICKINSON

Dust jacket for A 8.1.e

A 8.1.i
Ninth printing [1959]

New York: Harper & Brothers, [1959].

The copyright page reads 'K-I', indicating October 1959 printing.

Location: WU.

A 8.1.j
Tenth printing [1967]

New York, Evanston, and London: Harper & Row, [1967].

The copyright page reads 'C-R', indicating March 1967 printing.

Locations: IEN, MB.

A 8.1.k

New York: Dover, [1969].

Facsimile reprinting of A 8.1.d. Wrappers. Price, $3.00. DLC copy (bound) received 14 January 1970. *Locations:* MA, MAJ, RPB, White.

Note: There is an added note on p. 125 stating that poem 232 is by George Herbert, not Dickinson.

A 9 EMILY DICKINSON'S LETTERS TO DR. AND MRS. JOSIAH GILBERT HOLLAND

A 9.1.a
Only edition, first printing (1951)

Emily Dickinson's Letters

TO DR. AND MRS. JOSIAH GILBERT HOLLAND

EDITED BY THEIR GRANDDAUGHTER
THEODORA VAN WAGENEN WARD

HARVARD UNIVERSITY PRESS
CAMBRIDGE, MASSACHUSETTS
1951

A 9.1.a: 8¼″ × 5⁹⁄₁₆″

[i–iv] v–vii [viii–xii] [1–2] 3–27 [28–30] 31–64 [65–66] 67–79 [80–82] 83–98 [99–100] 101–157 [158–160] 161–201 [202] 203–226 [227–228] 229–252

[1–16⁸ 17⁴] Two single-leaf gatherings and a six-leaf gathering, all with illustrations, are inserted after pp. 148, 164, and 244, respectively.

Contents: p. i: '*Emily Dickinson's Letters* | TO DR. AND MRS. JOSIAH GILBERT HOLLAND'; p. ii: blank; p. iii: title page; p. iv: copyright page; pp. v–vii: 'PREFACE'; p. viii: blank; p. ix: contents; p. x: blank; p. xi: list of illustrations; p. xii: blank; p. 1: 'THE BACKGROUND'; p. 2: 12 lines of verse, beginning '*They shut me up in prose* —'; pp. 3–27: texts of letters; p. 28: blank; p. 29: 'PART ONE | 1853–1860'; p. 30: blank; pp. 31–64: texts of letters; p. 65: 'PART TWO | 1865–1868'; p. 66: blank; pp. 67–79: texts of letters; p. 80: blank; p. 81: 'PART THREE | 1870–1879'; p. 82: blank; pp. 83–98: texts of letters; p. 99: 'PART FOUR | 1875–1881'; p. 100: blank; pp. 101–148: texts of letters; inserted leaf with an engraving of Dickinson's home printed on the recto and photographs of Dr. and Mrs. Holland printed on the verso; p. 149–157: texts of letters; p. 158: blank; p. 159: 'PART FIVE | 1882–1886'; p. 160: blank; pp. 161–164: texts of letters; inserted leaf with photograph of Annie and Kate Holland printed on the recto and a photograph of Lavinia Dickinson printed on the verso; pp. 165–201: texts of letters; p. 202: blank; pp. 203–226: 'NOTES'; p. 227: 'APPENDICES'; p. 228: blank; pp. 229–230: 'APPENDIX A | Letters Published Previously'; pp. 231–232: 'APPENDIX B | Chronology of the Dickinson and Holland Families'; pp. 233–238: 'APPENDIX C | A Study of the Papers Used'; pp. 239–244: 'APPENDIX D | A Study of the Handwriting'; inserted six-leaf gathering, numbered pp. 1–12, with facsimiles of manuscript letters; pp. 245–246: 'INDEX OF POEMS'; pp. 247–252: 'GENERAL INDEX'.

Typography and paper: 6″ × 4″; wove paper, watermarked '[curved] WARREN'S | OLDE STYLE'; 31 lines per page. No running heads.

Binding: Light gray fine linen cloth with very deep red stamping; front cover: design of two flowers at bottom right; back cover: blank; spine: 'WARD | [from top to bottom] *Emily Dickinson's Letters* | HARVARD'. Wove endpapers. All edges trimmed.

Dust jacket: Light green-gray wove paper; front cover: '[deep red] *Emily Dickinson's Letters* | TO DR. AND MRS. JOSIAH GILBERT HOLLAND | [drawing of Dickinson's house] | EDITED BY THEODORA VAN WAGENEN WARD'; back cover: blurbs for three books; spine: 'WARD | [from top to bottom in deep red] *Emily Dickinson's Letters* | HARVARD'; front and back flaps: description of the book.

Publication: Advertised for 19 April 1951, in *Publishers Weekly* 159 (27 January 1951), advertising section. Listed in *Publishers Weekly* 159 (21 April 1951), 1746. Application for copyright received, 22 March 1951; books received, 23 March 1951. Copyright registration A53776. According to the publisher's records, published 19 April 1951. Deposit copy: DLC (23 March 1951). Inscribed copies: MA (April 1951), NjP (8 April 1951). NNC copy (rebound) received 24 April 1951; NjP copy received 7 May 1951; MBAt copy received 12 May 1951. Price, $4.00.

Printing: Printed by the Harvard University Printing Office; bound by the Norwood Press, Norwood, Mass.

$4.00

PUBLISHER'S NOTE

Emily Dickinson has been one of the most misunderstood and misrepresented of our American poets. The publication of this group of letters marks what we hope is the beginning of a genuinely historical approach to her life, her prose, and her poetry.

Ninety-three letters written by Emily Dickinson to Mrs. Ward's grandparents, Dr. and Mrs. Josiah Gilbert Holland, are published in this volume. They are intimate, unreserved, and at the same time characteristically poetic. In the seventeen-year span of revealing letters, Emily spoke freely to these close friends, particularly to Mrs. Holland, whom she called "Sister." The letters and the more than thirty poems, which were sometimes included with the letters and sometimes sent in place of them, span the major portion of Emily's adult life. They range from 1853, when she was a girl in her early twenties, full of hope and still immature, to 1886, the last year of her life, by which time she had come

Continued on back flap

Emily Dickinson's Letters

TO DR. AND MRS. JOSIAH GILBERT HOLLAND

EDITED BY THEODORA VAN WAGENEN WARD

WARD

Emily Dickinson's Letters

HARVARD

---

through more than one intense spiritual experience and the richness of her personality had reached its fullness.

Although the letters are allowed in large part to speak for themselves, Mrs. Ward's comments help to create a background for them by throwing light on personal allusions in their contents. A separate section of notes identifies the historical and literary allusions and quotations.

The letters are arranged chronologically according to a painstaking process of internal and external analysis which will be an aid in the preparation of future editions of Emily's letters and poems; a small appendix states succinctly and spaciously how the analysis of the paper and handwriting led to the present dating.

This is the first of the books made possible by the transfer of the Dickinson papers, and all rights connected with them, to the Houghton Library of Harvard University. Sixty-four letters and six poems are here published for the first time.

HARVARD UNIVERSITY PRESS
CAMBRIDGE 38, MASSACHUSETTS

HERMAN MELVILLE

Journal of a Visit to London and the Continent, 1849–1850

Edited by ELEANOR MELVILLE METCALF

"When Herman Melville went on board the Southampton, bound for London in October, 1849, he had reached the most creative period of his life . . . The record of that trip Melville wrote down in a journal now far out of print and long ago published . . . More than a record of a sharp impression of men and cities, it is a veritable medley of ideas, scenes, and characters which would germinate in his later works . . . Readers of Melville, who now are legion, will be grateful for this intimate view."—Willard Thorp, *The New York Herald Tribune Weekly Book Review.* $3.75

MELVILLE'S BILLY BUDD

Edited by F. BARRON FREEMAN

"One of the most important of recent Melville studies. It is important because it gives us for the first time a reliable text, because it offers incontrovertible evidence of Melville's normal method of composition (at least at that time) . . . and because, in a long introduction, Mr. Freeman explores all the kinds of sources that Melville used, and reconstructs, in both literal and psychological terms, the actual workings of Melville's creative imagination."—Robert E. Spiller, *Saturday Review of Literature.* $5.00

HERMAN MELVILLE
The Tragedy of Mind

By WILLIAM ELLERY SEDGWICK

"Mr. Sedgwick has added the keystone to the books on Melville that have been appearing ever since his revival in 1919. This is not just an-other biography, but a thoughtful attempt to comprehend the unfolding of a great writer's personality. It adds a distinguished item to the rapidly growing shelf of mature American literary criticism." — George F. Whicher, *The New York Herald Tribune.* $3.75

At all booksellers, or from

HARVARD UNIVERSITY PRESS
CAMBRIDGE 38, MASSACHUSETTS

Locations: CtY (dust jacket), DLC, ICN, IEN, JM (dust jacket), MA (dust jacket), MB, MBAt, MH, NN, NcD, NcU, NjP (two copies) (dust jacket), RPB, ViU (dust jacket), WU (dust jacket).

Note: Jacob Blanck reports that "inserted in some copies is an erratum slip referring to the copyright notice"; no such slips have been located (see *Bibliography of American Literature* 2:452).

A 9.1.b
Second printing (1951)

Cambridge, Mass.: Harvard University Press, 1951.

The same as the first printing, except: the copyright page reads 'COPYRIGHT 1896, BY ROBERTS BROTHERS. COPYRIGHT 1914, | 1924, 1929, 1935, 1942 BY MARTHA DICKINSON BIANCHI. | COPYRIGHT 1951, BY THE PRESIDENT AND FELLOWS OF | HARVARD COLLEGE. | *Second Printing* | [the last two lines are the same as in the first printing]'. Dust jacket. *Locations:* IEN, JM, MA.

A 10 THE POEMS OF EMILY DICKINSON

A 10.1.a
First edition, first printing (1955)

THE POEMS OF

Emily Dickinson

*Including variant readings critically compared
with all known manuscripts*

Edited by

THOMAS H. JOHNSON

*THE BELKNAP PRESS
of HARVARD UNIVERSITY PRESS
Cambridge, Massachusetts*
1 9 5 5

A 10.1.a: 9³/₁₆″ × 6⅛″; Dickinson's name and the lion are in medium red

Vol. I: [i–ix] x–xv [xvi] xvii–lxviii [i–ii] 1–378

Vol. II: [i–iv] [i–ii] 379–820

Vol. III: [i–vi] [i–ii] 821–1186 [1187–1188] 1189–1210 [1211–1212] 1213–1226 [1227–1228] 1229–1266 [1267–1268]

Vol. I: [1^8 2–14^{16} 15^8] A ten-leaf gathering of calendered paper or the same paper as the text containing facsimiles of manuscript poems is inserted after p. xlvii

Vol. II: [1^8 2–14^{16} 15^8]

Vol. III: [1^8 2–12^{16} 13^{20} 14^{16} 15^8]

Contents: Vol. I: p. i: 'THE POEMS OF EMILY DICKINSON | VOLUME I'; p. ii: blank; p. iii: title page; p. iv: copyright page; p. v: " 'If fame belonged to me, | I could not escape her." | *E. D. to T. W. H.* | *June 1862.'*; p. vi: blank; p. vii: 'FOREWORD', signed 'T.H.J.'; p. viii: blank; pp. ix–x: contents; pp. xi–xii: 'PUBLISHER'S PREFACE', signed 'THOMAS J. WILSON | *Director, Harvard University Press* | *June 1955'*; pp. xiii–xv: 'ACKNOWLEDGE-MENTS', signed '*Lawrenceville, New Jersey* THOMAS H. JOHNSON | *27 April 1955'*; p. xvi: blank; pp. xvii–xxxviii: 'CREATING THE POEMS'; pp. xxxix–xlviii: 'EDITING THE POEMS'; inserted ten-leaf gathering of coated paper with facsimiles of manuscript poems; pp. xlix–lix: 'CHARACTERISTICS OF THE | HANDWRITING'; pp. lx–lxviii: 'NOTES ON THE PRESENT TEXT'; p. i: 'POEMS | 1–494 | [1850–1862]'; p. ii: blank; pp. 1–378: poems; Vol. II: p. i: half title, the same as in Vol. I, except 'II'; p. ii: blank; p. iii: title page, the same as in Vol. I, except 'II'; p. iv: copyright page, the same as in Vol. I; p. i: 'POEMS | 495–1176 | [1862–1870]'; p. ii: blank; pp. 379–820: poems; Vol. III: p. i: half title, the same as in Vol. I, except 'III'; p. ii: blank; p. iii: title page, the same as in Vol. I, except 'III'; p. iv: copyright page, the same as in Vol. I; p. v: contents; p. vi: blank; p. i: 'POEMS | 1177–1775 | [1870–1886] | AND UNDATED POEMS'; p. ii: blank; pp. 821–1186: poems; p. 1187: 'APPENDICES'; p. 1188: blank; pp. 1189–1210: appendices; p. 1211: 'SUBJECT INDEX'; p. 1212: blank; pp. 1213–1226: subject index;

p. 1227: 'INDEX OF FIRST LINES'; p. 1228: blank; pp. 1229–1266: index of first lines; pp. 1267–1268: blank.

Typography and paper: 6⅝″ (6⅜″) × 4⁵⁄₁₆″; wove paper, watermarked '[curved] WARREN'S | OLDE STYLE'; 35 lines per page; various lines per page for poetry. Running heads: Vol. I: rectos: p. xv: 'ACKNOWLEDGEMENTS'; pp. xix–xxxvii: 'CREATING THE POEMS'; pp. xli–xlvii: 'EDITING THE POEMS'; pp. li–lix: 'CHARACTERISTICS OF THE HANDWRITING'; pp. lxi–lxvii: 'NOTES ON THE PRESENT TEXT'; versos: p. xii: 'PUBLISHER'S PREFACE'; p. xiv: 'ACKNOWLEDGEMENTS'; pp. xviii–lviii, lxii–lxviii: 'INTRODUCTION'; Vol. II: no running heads; Vol. III: rectos: pp. 1191–1205: 'APPENDIX' and number in arabic numerals; pp. 1215–1225: 'SUBJECT INDEX'; pp. 1231–1265: 'INDEX OF FIRST LINES'; versos: p. 1190–1200, 1204, 1208–1210: 'APPENDIX' and number in arabic numerals; pp. 1214–1226: 'SUBJECT INDEX'; pp. 1230–1266: 'INDEX OF FIRST LINES'.

Binding: Dark gray buckram; front and back covers: blank; spine: '[blackstamped ornamental band] | [goldstamped rule] | [six lines goldstamped on black background] THE | POEMS | OF | *Emily* | *Dickinson* | *JOHNSON* | [goldstamped rule] | [blackstamped ornamental band] | [blackstamped] I [II] [III] | [goldstamped lion] | [three lines blackstamped] *BELKNAP* | *PRESS* | *HARVARD*'. Stiff wove endpapers.

Box: Morocco grain deep red paper-covered cardboard box with a single white laid paper label on the spine and front: spine label reads 'THE POEMS OF | [deep red] *Emily Dickinson* | *Including variant readings critically compared* | *with all known manuscripts* | *Edited by* | *THOMAS H. JOHNSON*'; front part of label reads 'THE POEMS OF | [deep red] *Emily Dickinson* | *Edited by* | *THOMAS H. JOHNSON* | [deep red lion] | *THE BELKNAP PRESS* | *of HARVARD UNIVERSITY PRESS*'.

Review copy: Sewn, trimmed sheets bound in deep red stiff morocco grain paper wrappers (with white endpapers) with a label on each of the front wrappers that is the same as the back part of the label on the box and with the volume numbers hand-lettered in roman numerals on the spines. See *note*.

Publication: Listed in *Publishers Weekly* 168 (17 September 1955), 1320. Application for copyright received, 15 August 1955; books received, 18 August 1955. Copyright registration A206524. According to the publisher's records, published 12 September 1955. Deposit copy: DLC (18 August 1955). MBAt copy received 16 September 1955; MH copy received 21 September 1955. Price, $25.00 a set.

Printing: Printed by the Harvard University Printing Office; bound by the Stanhope Bindery, Boston.

Locations: CtY, DLC, ICN, IEN, JM (box), MA (box), MAJ (box), MB (box), MBAt, MH (box), NN, NcU, NjP (box), RPB, ViU (box), ViU (review copy), WU (box).

Note: A handwritten note on the only located review copy states, "Only 25 copies were bound in wrappers for review."

A 10.1.b
Second printing (1958)

Cambridge, Mass.: The Belknap Press of Harvard University Press, 1958.

The copyright page reads *'Second Printing'*. The inserted illustrations are on calendered paper. *Locations:* CtY, NN, NNC, NcD, NcU, WU.

Note: The second and subsequent reprintings contain a list of corrections on 3:1188.

A 10.1.c
Third printing (1963)

Cambridge, Mass.: The Belknap Press of Harvard University Press, 1963.

The copyright page reads 'Third Printing'. The inserted illustrations are on the same paper as the text, as is the case in subsequent reprintings. *Locations:* IEN, MB, NNC, ViU.

A 10.1.d
Fourth printing [1968]

Cambridge, Mass.: The Belknap Press of Harvard University Press, [1968].

The copyright page reads 'Fourth Printing 1968'. *Locations:* MB, NcD.

A 10.1.e
Fifth printing [1974]

Cambridge, Mass.: The Belknap Press of Harvard University Press, [1974].

The copyright page reads 'Fifth Printing, 1974'. *Location:* MAJ.

A 10.1.f
Sixth printing [1977]

Cambridge, Mass.: The Belknap Press of Harvard University Press, [1977].

Not seen.

A 10.1.g
Seventh printing [1979]

Cambridge, Mass.: The Belknap Press of Harvard University Press, [1979].

Not seen.

A 10.2.a
Second edition, first printing [1960]

THE COMPLETE POEMS OF | Emily Dickinson | [ornate rule] | EDITED BY | Thomas H. Johnson | [publisher's logo] | LITTLE, BROWN AND COMPANY | BOSTON   TORONTO

xiii, 770 pp. Dust jacket. The copyright page reads 'FIRST EDITION'. Price, $10.00. Deposit copy: DLC (27 October 1960). DLC copy (rebound) received 5 October 1960; MBAt copy received 31 October 1960. *Locations:* CtY, DLC, JM, MA, MAJ, MBAt, MH, NN, NcU, NjP, RPB, ScU, WU.

Note one: A slip is present before the title page in some copies: 'The publisher in presenting this volume acknowledges | permission of the President and Fellows of Harvard College | and of the Trustees of Amherst College'.

Note two: The following reprintings have been noted: 'THIRD PRINTING' (NNC— received 10 June 1965); 'FOURTH PRINTING' (NcU); 'FIFTH PRINTING' (IEN, MB); 'TENTH PRINTING' (NcU); 'THIRTEENTH PRINTING' (MB), 'FOURTEENTH PRINTING' (White), 'Fifteenth Printing' (White).

Note three: First reprinted in wrappers in [1976]. Price, $6.95. Reprintings with the following publisher's codes have been noted: 'A' (MAJ—received 12 March 1976), 'B' (RPB), 'E' (JM), 'G' (White), 'MV' (White).

A 10.2.b
Second printing for English sale [1970]

THE COMPLETE POEMS OF | Emily Dickinson | [ornate rule] | EDITED BY | Thomas H. Johnson | FABER AND FABER LIMITED | LONDON: 24 RUSSELL SQUARE

Dust jacket. The copyright page reads *'First published in England in 1970'*. Price: £4.20. Deposit copy: BL (12 January 1970). DLC copy received 27 April 1970. *Locations:* BL, DLC, MA, MAJ, NcU, NjP, RPB.

Note one: First reprinted in wrappers in [1975] at 84s. The following reprintings have been noted: [1975] (cloth, RPB, White; wrappers, BC, BO, White), [1977] (wrappers, JM, White).

Note two: A possible review copy has been noted bound in unprinted gray wrappers: White.

A 10.3.a
Only edition, first printing [1961]

Final Harvest | [ornate rule] | EMILY DICKINSON'S | —POEMS— | SELECTION AND INTRODUCTION BY | Thomas H. Johnson | [publisher's logo] | BOSTON · TORONTO | LITTLE, BROWN AND COMPANY

xvi, 331 pp. Dust jacket. Price, $4.75. Copyright, 6 December 1961. The copyright page reads 'FIRST EDITION'. Deposit copy: DLC (11 December 1961). Inscribed copy: NjP (15 January 1962). MA copy received 25 January 1962. *Locations:* DLC, IEN, JM, MA, MB, MH, NN, NjP, RPB, WU.

Note: "The text is that of the variorum Harvard Edition (1955) [A 10.1], as standardized in *The Complete Poems of Emily Dickinson* (Little, Brown and Company, 1960) [A 10.2]" (p. [321]).

A 10.3.b–aa
Second through twenty-seventh printings [n.d.]

Boston, Toronto: Little, Brown and Company, [n.d.].

Cloth or wrappers. The latest noted reprinting in cloth is the *'Eighth Printing'*. First reprinted in wrappers in [1964] as LB51 at $1.95. The latest noted reprinting in wrappers contains the publisher's code 'S'. *Locations:* cloth: 'SECOND PRINTING' (MA, NcU, NjP—received 18 September 1963); 'THIRD PRINTING' (NNC—received 10 March 1965); 'FIFTH PRINTING' (MB); 'SIXTH PRINTING' (IEN); 'SEVENTH PRINTING' (MH); *'Eighth Printing'* (NcU, ViU, White); wrappers: 'A' (NcU, NjP, RPB, ViU, WU); 'D' (JM); 'E' (MH); 'I' (JM); 'L' (NcU, White); 'N' (White); 'O' (White); 'P' (WU); 'R' (JM, White); 'S' (White).

A 11 THE LETTERS OF EMILY DICKINSON

A 11.1.a
First edition, first printing (1958)

THE LETTERS OF

Emily Dickinson

Edited by

THOMAS H. JOHNSON

Associate Editor

THEODORA WARD

THE BELKNAP PRESS
of HARVARD UNIVERSITY PRESS
Cambridge, Massachusetts

1958

A 11.1.a: 9³⁄₁₆″ × 6⅛″; Dickinson's name and the lion are in very deep red

Vol. I: [i–ii] [i–v] vi–vii [viii] ix–xiii [xiv] xv–xxvii [xxviii] [1–2] 3–41 [42–44] 45–71 [72–74] 75–105 [106–108] 109–312 [313–314]

Vol. II: [i–ii] [i–iv] v [vi] vii [viii] [313–314] 315–330 [331–332] 333–386 [387–388] 389–446 [447–448] 449–466 [467–468] 469–533 [534–536] 537–652 [653–654]

Vol. III: [i–ii] [i–iv] [v] vi [vii] viii [653–654] 655–805 [806–808] 809–908 [909–910] 911–929 [930–932] 933–974 [975–976] 977–993 [994] 995–999 [1000–1002]

Vol. I: [1–18^8 19^{12} 20^8] A two-leaf gathering of coated paper with photographs of varous people and places is inserted after p. 154

Vol. II: [1–22^8] Two two-leaf gatherings of coated paper with photographs of various people and manuscript letters are inserted after pp. 534 and 582.

Vol. III: [1–20^8 21^{12} 22^8] A two-leaf gathering of coated paper with photographs of various people is inserted after p. 778

Contents: Vol. I: pp. i–ii: blank; p. iii: 'THE LETTERS OF EMILY DICKINSON | VOLUME I'; p. ii: blank; p. iii: title page; p. iv: copyright page; pp. v–vii: contents; p. viii: blank; pp. ix–x: list of illustrations; pp. xi–xiii: "ACKNOWLEDGEMENTS', signed 'THOMAS H. JOHNSON | *Jaffrey, New Hampshire* | *August 1957*'; p. xiv: blank; pp. xv–xxii: 'INTRODUCTION'; pp. xxiii–xxvii: 'NOTES ON THE PRESENT TEXT'; p. xxviii: blank; p. 1: 'I | LETTERS | 1–14 | [1842–1846] | ". . . *the Hens* | *lay finely . . .*" '; p. 2: introduction; pp. 3–41: texts of letters; p. 42: blank; p. 43: 'II | LETTERS | 15–26 | [1847–1848] | "*I am really* | *at Mt Holyoke . . .*" '; p. 44: introduction; pp. 45–71: texts of letters; p. 72: blank; p. 73: 'III | LETTERS | 27–39 | [1849–1850] | "*Amherst is alive* | *with fun this winter . . .*" '; p. 74: introduction; pp. 75–105: texts of letters; p. 106: blank; p. 107: 'IV | LETTERS | 40–176 | [1851–1854] | ". . . *we do not have much poetry,* | *father having made up his mind* | *that its all pretty much* real life." '; p. 108: introduction; pp. 109–154: texts of letters; inserted two-leaf gathering of coated paper with photographs of two houses Dickinson lived in and Austin Dickinson, Susan Gilbert, Lavinia Norcross Dickinson, Martha Gilbert, James L. Graves, and Elizabeth Chapin Holland printed on both sides; pp. 155–312: texts of letters; pp. 313–314: blank; Vol. II: pp. i–ii: blank; p. i: half title, the same as in Vol. I, except 'II'; p. ii: blank; p. iii: title page, the same as in Vol. I, except 'II'; p. iv: copyright page, the same as in Vol. I; p. v: contents; p. vi: blank; p. vii: list of illustrations; p. viii: blank; p. 313: 'V | LETTERS | 177–186 | [1855–1857] | "*To live, and die, and mount* | *again in triumphant body . . .* | *is no schoolboy's theme!"* '; p. 314: introduction; pp. 315–330: texts of letters; p. 331: 'VI | LETTERS | 187–245 | [1858–1861] | *Much has occurred . . . so much —* | *that I stagger as I write,* *in* | *its sharp remembrance.*'; p. 332: introduction; pp. 333–386: texts of letters; p. 387: 'VII | LETTERS | 246–313 | [1862–1865] | *Perhaps you smile at me* | *I could not stop for* *that —* | *My Business is Circumference.*'; p. 388: introduction; pp. 389–466: texts of letters; p. 467: 'VIII | LETTERS | 314–337 | '1866–1869] | *A Letter always feels to me* | *like immortality because it is* | *the mind alone without corporeal friend.*'; p. 448: introduction; pp. 449–466: texts of letters; p. 467: 'IX | LETTERS | 338–431 | [1870–1874] | *I* *find ecstacy in living —* | *the mere sense of living* | *is joy enough.*'; p. 468: introduction; pp. 469–533: texts of letters; p. 534: blank; inserted two-leaf gathering of coated paper with photographs of Thomas Wentworth Higginson, Helen Hunt Jackson, Jonathan L. Jenkins, and Samuel Bowles (two) printed on both sides; p. 535: 'X | LETTERS | 432– 626 | [1875–1879] | *Nature is a Haunted House —* | *but Art — a House that tries to be* *haunted.*'; p. 536: introduction; pp. 537–582: texts of letters; inserted two-leaf gathering with photographs of four manuscript letters printed on both sides; pp. 583–662: texts of letters; pp. 653–654: blank; Vol. III: p. i–ii: blank; p. i: half title, the same as in Vol. I, except 'III'; p. ii: blank; p. iii: title page, the same as in Vol. I, except 'III'; p. iv: copyright page, the same as in Vol. I; p. v: contents; p. vi: blank; p. vii: list of illustrations; p. viii: blank; p. 653: 'XI | LETTERS | 627–878 | [1880–1883] | *I hesitate which word to take,* | *as I can take but few and each* | *must be the chiefest . . .*'; p. 654: introduction; pp. 655–778: texts of letters; inserted two-leaf gathering of coated paper with photographs of Otis P. Lord, Edward (Ned) Dickinson, Gilbert Dickinson, Martha Dickinson (two), Ned Dickinson and a friend, and the cast of "The Fair Barbarian" printed on both sides; pp. 779–805: texts of letters; p. 806: blank; p. 807: 'XII | LETTERS | 879–1045 | [1884–1886] | *. . . A Letter is a joy of Earth —* | *it is denied the Gods.*'; p. 808: introduction; pp. 809–906: texts of letters; pp. 907–908: 'ADDITIONAL LETTERS'; p. 909: 'PROSE FRAGMENTS'; p. 910: blank; pp. 911–929: texts of prose fragments; p. 930: blank; p. 931: 'APPENDICES'; p. 932: blank; pp. 933–958: 'APPENDIX 1 | BIO- GRAPHICAL SKETCHES OF RECIPIENTS OF LETTERS | AND OF PERSONS MEN- TIONED IN THEM'; pp. 959–960: 'APPENDIX 2 | A NOTE ON THE DOMESTIC HELP'; pp. 961–964: 'APPENDIX 3 | RECIPIENTS OF LETTERS'; p. 975: 'INDEX | INDEX OF POEMS'; p. 976: two lines of errata; pp. 977–993: index; p. 994: blank; pp. 995–999: index of poems; pp. 1000–1002: blank.

Typography and paper: 6^{15}⁄₁₆″ × 4⅜″; appendices, 6¾″ (6⁹⁄₁₆″) × 4⅜″; wove paper watermarked '[curved] WARREN'S | OLDE STYLE'; 38 lines per page; various lines per page for poetry. Running heads: Vol. I: no running heads; Vol. II: no running heads; Vol. III: rectos: pp. 935–957, 963–973: 'APPENDIX' and number in arabic numerals; pp. 979–993: 'INDEX'; pp. 997–999: 'INDEX OF POEMS'; versos: pp. 934–974: 'AP- PENDIX' and number in arabic numerals; pp. 978–992: 'INDEX'; pp. 996–998: 'INDEX OF POEMS'.

Binding: Dark blue buckram; front and back covers: blank; spine: goldstamped '[or- namental band] | [rule] | [six lines on deep red background] THE | LETTERS | OF | *Emily* | *Dickinson* | *JOHNSON* | [rule] | [ornamental band] | I [II] [III] | [lion] | *BELKNAP* | *PRESS* | *HARVARD*'. Wove endpapers. All edges trimmed.

Box: Dark grey paper-covered cardboard box with a single white laid paper label on the spine and front: spine reads 'THE LETTERS OF | [deep red] *Emily Dickinson* | *Edited by* | *THOMAS H. JOHNSON* | *Associate Editor* | *THEODORA WARD* | [deep red lion] | *THE BELKNAP PRESS* | *of HARVARD UNIVERSITY PRESS*'; front part of label reads 'THE LETTERS OF | [deep red] *Emily Dickinson* | [photograph of Dickinson] | *THE BELKNAP PRESS* | *of HARVARD UNIVERSITY PRESS* | THREE VOLUMES BOXED $25.00'.

Publication: Advertised for 17 March 1958, in *Publishers Weekly* 173 (27 January 1958), advertising section. Listed in *Publishers Weekly* 173 (24 March 1958), 60. Application for copyright received, 10 March 1958; books received, 10 February 1958. Published 17 March 1958. Copyright registration A330508. Deposit copy: DLC (10 February 1958). Inscribed copy: CtY (March 1958). MBAt copy received 12 March 1958; MH copy received 13 March 1958; MAJ copy received 14 March 1958; MA copy received 17 March 1958; another MH copy received 25 March 1958. Price, $25.00 a set.

Printing: Printed by the Harvard University Printing Office; bound by the Stanhope Bindery, Boston.

Locations: CtY, DLC, ICN, IEN, InU (box), JM (box), MA (box), MAJ (box), MB (box), MBAt, MH (two copies) (box), NN, NNC, NcD, NcU, NjP (box), RPB, ScU, ViU, WU.

Note: Listed as an importation by Oxford University Press for 8 May 1958 in the *English Catalogue* at 200s. a set.

A 11.1.b
Second printing (1965)

Cambridge, Mass.: The Belknap Press of Harvard University Press, 1965.

The copyright page reads '*Second Printing*'. The illustrations are on the same paper as the text, as is the case in all subsequent reprintings. *Locations:* IEN, NcD.

A 11.1.c
Third printing [1970]

Cambridge, Mass.: The Belknap Press of Harvard University Press, [1970].

The copyright page reads '*Third printing, 1970*'. *Locations:* CtY, JM, NcU, WU.

A 11.1.d
Fourth printing [1976]

Cambridge, Mass.: The Belknap Press of Harvard University Press, [1976].

The copyright page reads '*Fourth printing, 1976*'. *Locations:* MB, MH.

A 11.1.e
Fifth printing [1979]

Cambridge, Mass.: The Belknap Press of Harvard University Press, [1979].

The copyright page reads '*Fifth printing, 1979*'. *Location:* MH.

A 11.2
Second edition, only printing (1971)

[two lines in script] Emily Dickinson | Selected Letters | EDITED BY THOMAS H. JOHNSON | THE BELKNAP PRESS | OF HARVARD UNIVERSITY PRESS | CAMBRIDGE, MASSACHUSETTS | 1971

xix, 364 pp. Dust jacket. Price, $10.00. Published 8 February 1971. Deposit copies: DLC (11 January 1971), two copies. MH copy received 4 February 1971; another MH copy received 11 February 1971; MBAt copy received 18 February 1971. *Locations:* CtY, DLC, JM, MAJ, MB, MBAt, MH, NNC, NcD, NcU, NjP, RPB, ViU.

A 12 THE MANUSCRIPT BOOKS OF EMILY DICKINSON

A 12.1
Only edition, only printing (1981)

THE MANUSCRIPT BOOKS OF

Emily Dickinson

VOLUME 1

Edited by R. W. Franklin

The Belknap Press of Harvard University Press

Cambridge, Massachusetts, and London, England · 1981

A 12.1: 9^{15}/₁₆″ × 6^{7}/₁₆″

Vol. I: [i–ix] x–xxii [i–ii] 1–692 [693] 694–706 [a–f]

Vol. II: [i–vi] [i–ii] 707–1157 [1158] 1159–1380 [1381] 1382–1442

Vol. I: [1–46^8]

Vol. II: [1–46^8]

Contents: Vol. I: p. i: 'The Manuscript Books of Emily Dickinson'; p. ii: blank; p. iii: title
page; p. iv: copyright page; p. v: 'Acknowledgements'; p. vi: blank; p. vii: contents; p.
viii: blank; pp. ix–xxii: 'Introduction'; p. i: 'Fascicles 1–29'; p. ii: blank; pp. 1–18:
Fascicle 1; pp. 19–36: Fascicle 2; pp. 37–54: Fascicle 3; pp. 55–72: Fascicle 4; pp.
73–90: Fascicle 5; pp. 91–108: Fascicle 6; pp. 109–126: Fascicle 7; pp. 127–148:
Fascicle 8; pp. 149–176: Fascicle 9; pp. 177–198: Fascicle 10; pp. 199–224: Fascicle
11; pp. 225–256: Fascicle 12; pp. 257–282: Fascicle 13; pp. 283–306: Fascicle 14;
pp. 307–332: Fascicle 15; pp. 333–352: Fascicle 16; pp. 353–378: Fascicle 17; pp.
379–406: Fascicle 18; pp. 407–432: Fascicle 19; pp. 433–454: Fascicle 20; pp. 455–
480: Fascicle 21; pp. 481–506: Fascicle 22; pp. 507–532: Fascicle 23; pp. 533–560:
Fascicle 24; pp. 561–586: Fascicle 25; pp. 587–612: Fascicle 26; pp. 613–638: Fasci-
cle 27; pp. 639–666: Fascicle 28; pp. 667–692: Fascicle 29; p. 693: 'Notes'; p. 694: list
of abbreviations; pp. 695–706: notes; pp. a–f: blank; Vol. II: p. i: half title, the same as
in Vol. I; p. ii: blank; p. iii: title page, the same as in Vol. I, except '2'; p. iv: copyright
page, the same as in Vol. I; p. v: contents; p. vi: blank; p. i: 'Fascicles 30–40 | Sets 1–

15'; p. ii: blank; pp. 707–732: Fascicle 30; pp. 733–758: Fascicle 31; pp. 759–784: Fascicle 32; pp. 785–810: Fascicle 33; pp. 811–836: Fascicle 34; pp. 837–868: Fascicle 35; pp. 869–894: Fascicle 36; pp. 895–920: Fascicle 37; pp. 921–946: Fascicle 38; pp. 947–972: Fascicle 39; pp. 973–998: Fascicle 40; pp. 999–1008: Set 1; pp. 1009–1014: Set 2; pp. 1015–1020: Set 3; pp. 1021–1030: Set 4; pp. 1031–1072: Set 5; pp. 1073—1152: Set 6; pp. 1153–1262: Set 7; pp. 1263–1308: Set 8; pp. 1309–1314: Set 9; pp. 1315–1332: Set 10; pp. 1333–1342: Set 11; pp. 1343–1348: Set 12; pp. 1349–1354: Set 13; pp. 1355–1376: Set 14; pp. 1377–1380: Set 15; p. 1381: 'Notes | Appendixes | Indexes'; p. 1382: list of abbreviations; pp. 1383–1390: notes; pp. 1391–1418: appendixes; pp. 1419–1442: indexes.

Typography and paper: $7\frac{1}{4}'' \times 4\frac{1}{2}''$ (various sizes for manuscript facsimiles); calendered wove paper; 40 lines per page, various lines per page for textual commentary and in manuscript facsimiles. No running heads (but see *note two*).

Binding: Grayish-brown buckram spine, extending over to meet paper-covered boards of brownish pink background with deep red diamond pattern (with rosette-like design on each corner and dot in center) on front and back covers; front and back covers: blank; spine: goldstamped '[rule] | FRANKLIN | [rule] | THE | MANUSCRIPT | BOOKS OF | Emily Dickinson | [rule] | 1 [2] | [rule] | BELKNAP | HARVARD'. Medium purplish red endpapers. All edges trimmed.

Box: Gray reddish brown fine linen cloth-covered cardboard box open at one end, with brownish pink label on spine: '[all within a single-rule frame] THE | MANUSCRIPT BOOKS | OF | [three lines in deep red] Emily | Dickinson | [leaf design] | Edited by R. W. Franklin'.

Publication: 2,500 copies. Published 22 December 1981. Price, $100 a set.

Printing: Printed by Meriden Gravure, Meriden, Conn.; bound by Halliday, West Hannover, Mass.

Locations: JM (box), MH (box), ScU, White (box).

Note one: Slips containing facsimiles of partial manuscript pages, printed on both sides, are tipped to the following pages: Vol. I: pp. 121, 352, 424; Vol. II: pp. 1052, 1115, 1148.

Note two: Rather than using running heads, this book employs various marginal tags to provide information about the facsimiles: "Manuscript numbers appear at the top of facsimile pages the first time applicable; they are not repeated. The variorum poem numbers are displayed in the outer margin at the beginning of poems. Symbols in the inner margin—occasionally in others—indicate the structure of the manuscript reproduced. For the usual sheet of two leaves, four pages, the symbols are: [open parenthesis for first recto, dashes for first verso and second recto, and closed parenthesis for second verso] Or, if the leaves are no longer conjugate: [open parenthesis to the left of broken line for first recto, dash to the right of broken line for first verso, dash to the left of broken line for second recto, and closed parenthesis to the right of broken line for second verso] . . . The broken line also appears alone—for a half-sheet used independently . . . and, in general, for edges torn or cut. A solid vertical line in the inner margin indicates a manufacturer's trim edge . . . ; other margins, except as noted, may be assumed to represent the original trim" (p. xx).

B. Miscellaneous Collections

All miscellaneous collections of Dickinson's writings in English through 1982, including bilingual collections, arranged chronologically.

B 1 THE COMPLETE POEMS OF EMILY DICKINSON
1924

B 1.1.a
Only edition, first printing (1924)

Two issues have been noted:

B 1.1.a₁
First (American) issue (1924)

[all within an ornamental frame] THE COMPLETE POEMS | OF | EMILY DICKINSON | WITH AN INTRODUCTION | BY HER NIECE | MARTHA DICKINSON BIANCHI | [publisher's logo] | BOSTON | LITTLE, BROWN, AND COMPANY | 1924

xiii, 330 pp. Dust jacket. 2,000 copies printed 2 July 1924. Advertised for 14 June 1924 at $3.00, in *Publishers Weekly* 105 (8 March 1924), 761; for fall 1924 at $3.50, in *Publishers Weekly* 105 (24 May 1924), 1641; for 2 July 1924, in *Publishers Weekly* 105 (28 June 1924), 1992. Listed in *Publishers Weekly* 106 (12 July 1924), 130. Price, $3.50. Application for copyright received, 24 July 1924; deposit copies received, 3 July 1924. The copyright page reads 'Published July, 1924'. Published 2 July 1924.

Locations: DLC (3 July 1924), NN (24 July 1924), CtY, ICN, IEN, JM, MA, MAJ, MH, NjP, RPB, ScU, ViU, WU.

Note: A set of galley proofs has been noted: MH.

B 1.1.a₂
Second (English) issue (1924)

[all within a single-rule frame surrounding an ornamental frame] THE COMPLETE POEMS | *of* | EMILY DICKINSON | WITH AN INTRODUCTION BY | MARTHA DICKINSON BIANCHI | LONDON | MARTIN SECKER | 1924

Amerincan sheets with a cancel title leaf. The copyright page reads '*All Rights Reserved* | London : Martin Secker Ltd., 1924'. Dust jacket (dated 1925). Published March 1925. Price, 21s.

Locations: BL (16 June 1925), BO (17 July 1925), CtY, MA, MAJ, NjP, RPB.

Note: The Complete Poems of Emily Dickinson contains *Poems, Poems: Second Series, Poems: Third Series,* and *The Single Hound,* plus five additional poems: "Title divine is mine" (pp. 176–177), "Through lane it lay, through bramble" (p. 297), "The Bible is an antique volume" (p. 299; rpt. from *Life and Letters* [C 7], pp. 91–92), "A little overflowing word" (p. 311; rpt. from *Life and Letters* [C 7], p. 80), and "Give little anguish, lives will fret" (p. 313). Mrs. Bingham suggests that Dickinson's poems were collected at this time because the copyright for *Poems: Third Series* would expire in

1924, and it was just as easy to collect all the poems as it was to renew the copyright on just one volume (*Ancestors' Brocades,* p. 385).

B 1.1.b
Second printing (1924)

Boston: Little, Brown, and Company, 1924.

1,000 copies printed 8 September 1924.

B 1.1.c
Third printing (1925)

Boston: Little, Brown, and Company, 1925.

2,000 copies printed 3 November 1924. *Locations:* JM, MA, MH, White.

B 1.1.d
Fourth printing (1926)

THE COMPLETE | POEMS of | EMILY DICKINSON | WITH AN INTRODUCTION | BY HER NIECE | MARTHA DICKINSON BIANCHI | BOSTON | LITTLE, BROWN, AND COM-PANY | 1926

xv, 330 pp. Flexible leather-covered boards; all edges gilded; white silk ribbon marker. Unprinted glassine dust jacket. Boxed. *Pocket Edition.* The same as the trade printing (B 1.1.a), except: pp. xi–xiii: "Introductory Note for the Pocket Edition," dated 3 May 1926; p. xv: contents. 2,000 copies printed 11 October 1926. *Locations:* MH (October 1926), MA (30 October 1926), MAJ, ViU, WU, White.

B 1.1.e
Fifth printing (1927)

Boston: Little, Brown, and Company, 1927.

Locations: RPB (5 February 1927), MAJ, MB, White.

B 1.1.f
Sixth printing (1928)

Two issues have been noted:

B 1.1.f$_1$
First (American) issue (1928)

Boston: Little, Brown, and Company, 1928.

Pocket Edition. 1,000 copies printed. *Not seen.*

B 1.1.f$_2$
Second (English) issue (1928)

London: Martin Secker, 1928.

American sheets with a cancel title leaf. Flexible cloth-covered boards; all edges gilded; blue silk ribbon marker. Dust jacket. *Pocket Edition.* Published December 1928. Price, 10s. 6d. *Locations:* BO, CtY, MAJ, NjP, RPB.

B 1.1.g
Seventh printing (1929)

Boston: Little, Brown, and Company, 1929.

Location: RPB.

B 1.1.h
Eighth printing (1929)

Boston: Little, Brown, and Company, 1929.

Pocket Edition. Boxed. *Locations:* MB, MH, PSt, RPB, WU.

B 1.1.i
Ninth printing (1930)

Boston, Little, Brown, and Company, 1930.

Locations: MB (25 June 1930), JM.

Note: Klaus Lubbers estimates the total printing of *Complete Poems* at 12,500 copies (*Emily Dickinson: The Critical Revolution* [Ann Arbor: University of Michigan Press, 1968], p. 248).

            B 2 SELECTED POEMS OF EMILY DICKINSON
                 1924

B 2.1.a
Only edition, first printing [1924]

[ornate capitals] *SELECTED POEMS* | *of* | [ornate capitals] *EMILY DICKINSON* | [publisher's logo] | *Edited by* | *CONRAD AIKEN* | *JONATHAN CAPE LTD* | *Eleven Gower Street London*

272 pp. Dust jacket. The copyright page reads 'FIRST PUBLISHED IN MCMXXIV'. Published September 1924. Price, 6s. *Locations:* BO (September 1924), BL (18 September 1924), CtY, FU, ICN, JM, MA, MAJ, MH, NNC, NjP, RPB, ViU, WU.

B 2.1.b
Second printing [1933]

London: Jonathan Cape, [1933].

The copyright page reads 'REPRINTED MCMXXXIII'. *Location:* CU.

            B 3 EMILY DICKINSON
                 1927

B 3.1
Only edition, only printing [1927]

[all within an ornate frame] EMILY DICKINSON | [rule] | [four lines within two parallel vertical rules] [two lines within an oval frame] · THE · | PAMPHLET POETS | *Price 25 cents* | [publisher's logo] | [rule] | SIMON & SCHUSTER : *PUBLISHERS* | *NEW YORK:* 37 WEST FIFTY-SEVENTH STREET

30 pp. Cover title. *The Pamphlet Poets.* Edited by Louis Untermeyer. Price, 25¢. Copyright, 16 May 1927. *Locations:* MB (24 May 1927), RPB (26 May 1927), DLC (27 May 1927), CtY, IEN, JM, MA, MAJ, MB, MH, NN, NNC, ViU, WU.

B 4 THE POEMS OF EMILY DICKINSON   CENTENARY EDITION
        1930

B 4.1.a
First edition, first printing (1930)

[green design] THE POEMS OF [green design] | EMILY DICKINSON | *Edited by* |
MARTHA DICKINSON BIANCHI | *and* ALFRED LEETE HAMPSON | [green script] Cen-
tenary Edition | [publisher's logo] | LITTLE, BROWN, AND COMPANY | [green design]
BOSTON   1930 [green design]

xv, 401 pp. Dust jacket. *Centenary Edition.* 5,025 copies printed 24 October 1930.
Advertised for 7 Novermber 1930 in *Publishers Weekly* 118 (20 September 1930),
1178. Listed in *Publishers Weekly* 118 (6 December 1930), 2559. Price, $4.00. Applica-
tion for copyright received, 25 November 1930; deposit copies received, 25 November
1930. Copyright renewed, 21 November 1957. The copyright page reads 'Published
November, 1930'. Published 21 November 1930.

Locations: CtY (18 November 1930), MAJ (20 November 1930), DLC (25 November
1930), ICN, JM, MA, MH, NN, NNC, NjP, RPB, WU.

Note one: A set of unbound, unsewn, folded and gathered sheets has been noted:
NjP.

Note two: *The Poems of Emily Dickinson* contains *Poems, Poems: Second Series,
Poems: Third Series, The Single Hound,* and *Further Poems.* The only first printing is of
"Fitter to see him I may be" (p. 276).

B 4.1.b
Second printing (1931)

Boston: Little, Brown, and Company, 1931.

The copyright page reads 'Reprinted, March 1931'. 3,035 copies printed 2 April 1931.
Locations: MA (15 June 1931), JM, MAJ, NjP, White.

B 4.1.c
Third printing (1932)

Boston: Little, Brown, and Company, 1932.

Locations: CtY, JM.

B 4.1.d
Fourth printing for English sale (1933)

[all within a single-rule frame surrounding a green ornamental frame] DEFINITIVE
COMPLETE EDITION | THE POEMS OF | EMILY DICKINSON | EDITED BY | MARTHA
DICKINSON BIANCHI | AND ALFRED LEETE HAMPSON | LONDON | MARTIN SECKER
| 1933

The copyright page reads "This edition . . . first published in England 1933". *Definitive
Complete Edition.* The same as the first printing, except: "Introduction" is not present.
Published October 1933. Price, 15s. *Locations:* BL (1 December 1933), BO (8 Decem-
ber 1933), OU, White.

B 4.1.e
Fifth printing (1934)

Boston: Little, Brown, and Company, 1934.

Locations: JM, MA, MH, WU.

B 4.1.f
Sixth printing (1935)

Boston: Little, Brown, and Company, 1935.

Location: CtY.

B 4.2.a
Second edition, first printing (1937)

Two issues have been noted:

B 4.2.a₁
First (American) issue (1937)

[all within an ornate green frame] *The Poems of* | EMILY DICKINSON | EDITED BY | MARTHA DICKINSON BIANCHI | AND | ALFRED LEETE HAMPSON | [green publisher's logo] | *Introduction by* | ALFRED LEETE HAMPSON | BOSTON | LITTLE, BROWN AND COMPANY | 1937

xv, 484 pp. Advertised as a "new one-volume edition" for 26 February 1937 in *Publishers Weekly* 131 (2 January 1937), 18; as an "enlarged edition" for February 1937 at $3.50 in *Publishers Weekly* 131 (30 January 1937), 432. Listed at $3.50 in *Publishers Weekly* 131 (27 February 1937), 1038. Price, $4.00. Application for copyright received, 27 February 1937; deposit copies received, 27 February 1937. The copyright page reads 'Published February, 1937'. Published 26 February 1937.

Locations: MAJ (26 February 1937), DLC (27 February 1937), CtY, ICN, MB, NN, NNC, NcU, ViU.

Note: *The Poems of Emily Dickinson* contains *Poems, Poems: Second Series, Poems: Third Series, The Single Hound, Further Poems,* and *Unpublished Poems.*

B 4.2.a₂
Second (English) issue [1937]

The Poems of | EMILY DICKINSON | EDITED BY | MARTHA DICKINSON BIANCHI | AND | ALFRED LEETE HAMPSON | *With an Introduction by* | ALFRED LEETE HAMPSON | [publisher's logo] | JONATHAN CAPE | THIRTY BEDFORD SQUARE | LONDON

American sheets with a cancel title leaf. The copyright page reads 'FIRST PUBLISHED 1937'. Published September 1937. Price, 12s. 6d. Bound by A. W. Bain & Co., London.

Locations: BL (9 September 1937), BO (15 September 1937), MAJ (25 October 1937), CaOTY, WU.

B 4.2.b
Second printing (1938)

Boston: Little, Brown and Company, 1938.

The copyright page reads 'Reprinted December, 1938'. *Locations:* JM, NjP.

B 4.2.c
Third printing (1939)

Boston: Little, Brown and Company, 1939.

The copyright page reads 'Reprinted November, 1939'. *Locations:* JM, NcD, White.

B 4.2.d
Fourth printing (1941)

Boston: Little, Brown and Company, 1941.

The copyright page reads 'Reprinted April, 1941'. *Locations:* MH, NcU, ViU, WU.

B 4.2.e
Fifth printing (1942)

Boston: Little, Brown and Company, 1942.

The copyright page reads 'Reprinted September, 1942'. *Location:* RPB.

B 2.4.f
Sixth printing (1943)

Boston: Little, Brown and Company, 1943.

The copyright page reads 'Reprinted August, 1943'. *Not seen.*

B 4.2.g
Seventh printing (1944)

Boston: Little, Brown and Company, 1944.

The copyright page reads 'Reprinted February, 1944'. *Locations:* JM, MA.

B 4.2.h
Eighth printing (1944)

Boston: Little, Brown and Company, 1944.

The copyright page reads 'Reprinted August, 1944'. *Location:* NcD.

B 4.2.i
Ninth printing (1945)

Boston: Little, Brown and Company, 1945.

The copyright page reads 'Reprinted December, 1945'. *Locations:* IEN, JM, White.

Note: The title page for this and subsequent reprintings reads '*Poems by* | EMILY . . .'.

B 4.2.j
Tenth printing (1946)

Boston: Little, Brown and Company, 1946.

The copyright page reads 'Reprinted October, 1946'. *Location:* MA (13 January 1947).

B 4.2.k

Boston: Little, Brown and Company, 1947.

The copyright page reads 'Reprinted April, 1947'. *Locations:* MB (24 February 1948), MH.

B 4.2.l

London: Jonathan Cape, [1947].

The copyright page reads 'FIRST PUBLISHED 1937 | *Reprinted 1947'*. Listed for September 1947 in the *English Catalogue*. *Location:* TxU (10 December 1947).

B 4.2.m

Boston: Little, Brown and Company, 1948.

The copyright reads 'Reprinted April, 1948'. *Location:* JM.

B 4.2.n

London: Jonathan Cape, [1948].

Location: RPB.

B 4.2.o

Boston: Little, Brown and Company, 1950.

The copyright page reads 'Reprinted May, 1950'. *Locations:* JM, MA, MAJ.

B 4.2.p

Boston: Little, Brown and Company, [1952].

The copyright page reads 'Reprinted May, 1952'. *Locations:* MH, NNC, NjP.

B 4.2.q

Boston: Little, Brown and Company, [1954].

The copyright page reads 'Reprinted February, 1954'. *Location:* NcU.

B 4.2.r

Boston: Little, Brown and Company, [1956].

The copyright page reads 'Reprinted January, 1956'. *Location:* NNC.

B 4.2.s–dd

Boston: Little, Brown and Company, [n.d.].

The copyright page has a copyright renewal notice dated 1957. The latest noted reprinting is the *'Thirtieth Printing'*. Locations: 'NINETEENTH PRINTING' (NjP); 'TWENTY-SECOND PRINTING' (White); 'TWENTY-THIRD PRINTING' (JM); 'TWENTY-FOURTH PRINTING' (MB, NcU); 'TWENTY-SEVENTH PRINTING' (White); 'TWENTY-NINTH PRINTING' (White); *'Thirtieth Printing'* (ScU).

                    B 5 POEMS FOR YOUTH
                         1934

B 5.1.a
Only edition, first printing (1934)

EMILY DICKINSON | [design] | [two lines in ornate capitals] POEMS | FOR YOUTH | EDITED BY | ALFRED LEETE HAMPSON | FOREWORD BY | MAY LAMBERTON

BECKER | ILLUSTRATIONS BY | GEORGE *and* DORIS HAUMAN | [drawing of girl with box inside of vines] | *Boston*   1934 | LITTLE, BROWN, AND COMPANY

Unpaged (60 leaves). Dust jacket. Price, $2.00. Published 23 November 1954. Copyright, 23 November 1934; copyright renewed, 21 September 1962. The copyright page reads 'Published November, 1934'.

Locations: DLC (27 November 1934), MAJ (4 December 1934), MA (12 December 1934), CtY, JM, MB, MH, NNC, NjP, RPB.

B 5.1.b
Second printing (1935)

Boston: Little, Brown, and Company, 1935.

The copyright page reads 'Reprinted July, 1935'. *Location:* WU.

B 5.1.c
Third printing (1936)

Boston: Little, Brown, and Company, 1936.

The copyright page reads 'Reprinted June, 1936'. *Not seen.*

B 5.1.d
Fourth printing (1936)

Boston: Little, Brown, and Company, 1936.

The copyright page reads 'Reprinted November, 1936'. *Location:* WU.

B 5.1.e
Fifth printing (1938)

Boston: Little, Brown and Company, 1938.

The copyright page reads 'Reprinted October, 1938'. *Locations:* CLU, MH.

B 5.1.f
Sixth printing (1940)

Boston: Little, Brown and Company, 1940.

The copyright page reads 'Reprinted August, 1940'. *Not seen.*

B 5.1.g
Seventh printing (1942)

Boston: Little, Brown and Company, 1942.

The copyright page reads 'Reprinted November, 1942'. *Location:* OCIW.

B 5.1.h
Eighth printing (1948)

Boston: Little, Brown and Company, 1948.

The copyright page reads 'Reprinted May, 1948'. *Not seen.*

B 5.1.i–m
Ninth through thirteenth printings [n.d.]

Boston: Little, Brown and Company, [n.d.].

Not seen.

B 5.1.n

Boston: Little, Brown and Company, 1950.

The copyright page reads *'Fourteenth Printing'. Location:* White.

B 5.1.o–x

Boston: Little, Brown and Company, [n.d.].

The latest noted reprinting is the 'TWENTY-FOURTH PRINTING'. *Locations:* 'TWENTY-FIRST PRINTING' (JM, White); 'TWENTY-THIRD PRINTING' (MAJ); 'TWENTY-FOURTH PRINTING' (NNC—2 June 1977, ScU).

B 6 TEN POEMS
1939

B 6.1
Only edition, only printing [1939]

TEN POEMS | *by* | EMILY DICKINSON | *1830–1886*

Unpaged (11 leaves). Wrappers. Published in Holland by the '5 lb press'. Selected and translated by Rosey E. Pool. Calligraphy by Susanne Heynemann. English and German on facing pages.

Locations: NN, RPB.

B 7 SELECTED POEMS
1940

B 7.1
Only edition, only printing (1940)

SELECTED POEMS | *by* | EMILY DICKINSON | [publisher's logo] | A. A. BALKEMA | 1940

70 pp. Wrappers. Published in Amsterdam. Edited by S. Vestdijk. Limited to 200 copies.

Locations: CtY, DLC, IEN, InU, MA, MAJ, RPB, ViU.

B 8 CHOIX DE POÈMES
1945

B 8.1
Only edition, only printing [1945]

EMILY DICKINSON | CHOIX DE POÈMES | TRADUCTION FRANÇAISE ET INTRODUC-
TION DE | FÉLIX ANSERMOZ-DUBOIS | ÉDITIONS DU CONTINENT | GENÈVE

126 pp. Self-wrappers with white printed band. Unprinted glassine dust jacket. Pub-
lished 31 October 1945. English and French on facing pages. Limited to 995 num-

bered copies: five for the editor, copies numbered I–XL and 1–900; and 50 unnumbered copies.

Locations: DLC (29 August 1946), CtY, MA, NcU, NjP.

B 9 POESIE
1945?

B 9.1
Only edition, only printing [1945?]

Emily Dickinson | POESIE | a cura di Marta Bini | M. A. DENTI EDITORE

xix, 203 pp. Wrappers. Dust jacket. Published in Milan. English and Italian on facing pages. Limited to 2,737 numbered copies, numbered I–CLXXII, 1–2565.

Locations: MA, RPB.

B 10 AN EMILY DICKINSON YEAR BOOK
1948

B 10.1.a
Only edition, first printing (1948)

Two issues have been noted:

A 10.1.a$_1$
First issue

An | Emily Dickinson | Year Book | *Edited by* | HELEN H. ARNOLD | *Drawings by* | LOUISE B. GRAVES | [gray-green handcolored circular design] | 1948 | THE HAMPSHIRE BOOKSHOP | Northampton, Massachusetts

xii, 132 pp. Dust jacket. Limited to 100 copies, signed and numbered by the editor and illustrator. The leaf containing the statement of limitation is tipped-in before the half title. Price, $5.00. Copyright, 15 May 1948.

Locations: MAJ (2 June 1948), MA, NjP.

A 10.1.a$_2$
Second issue

Northampton, Mass.: The Hampshire Bookshop, 1948.

The same as the first issue, except: the leaf containing the statement of limitation is not present; the circular design on the title page is not hand-colored. Dust jacket. Price, $3.50.

Locations: DLC (21 May 1948), IEN, JM, MA, MAJ, MBAt, MH, NjP, RPB, ViU, WU.

B 10.1.b
Second printing [1976]

[Folcroft, Pa.]: Folcroft Library Editions, 1976.

Facsimile reprinting of B 10.1.a$_2$. Limited to 100 copies. *Location:* DLC (24 May 1977).

Front cover of dust jacket for B 9

B 10.1.c
Third printing [1977]

[Norwood, Pa.: Norwood Editions, 1977].

Facsimile reprinting of B 10.1.a$_2$. *Locations:* DLC, NcU.

B 11 SELECTED POEMS OF EMILY DICKINSON
1948

B 11.1.a
Only edition, first printing [1948]

SELECTED POEMS | *of* | Emily Dickinson | *with an introduction by* CONRAD AIKEN |
[publisher's logo to the right of the next three lines] THE | MODERN LIBRARY | NEW
YORK | [rule]

xvi, 231 pp. Dust jacket. *The Modern Library* 25. Price, $1.25. The copyright page
reads 'FIRST MODERN LIBRARY EDITION 1948'.

Locations: NNC (1 December 1948), DLC (15 March 1949), CSt, MAJ, NN, NjP, RPB.

Note one: Numerous subsequent undated reprintings, all lacking the copyright page
reading.

Note two: The introduction by Aiken is reprinted from *Selected Poems* (B 2).

B 12 POEMS OF EMILY DICKINSON
1952

B 12.1.a
Only edition, first printing (1952)

[all within a box formed by the intersection of two parallel vertical brown rules and
double parallel horizontal brown rules at the top, and parallel double horizontal brown
rules at the bottom] *Poems of* | *Emily Dickinson* | SELECTED AND EDITED | WITH A
COMMENTARY BY | LOUIS UNTERMEYER | AND ILLUSTRATED | WITH DRAWINGS
BY | HELEN SEWELL | [star] | *New York, The Limited Editions Club* | 1952

xxviii, 286 pp. Unprinted glassine dust jacket. Full leather. Boxed. Limited to 1,500
numbered copies, signed by the illustrator. Copyright, 10 November 1952.

Locations: DLC (18 November 1952), MB (18 November 1952), NN (28 November
1952), IEN, JM, MA, MH, NNC, NjP, RPB, WU.

B 12.1.b
Second printing [1952]

New York: The Heritage Press, [1952].

The American Poets. Boxed. Unprinted glassine dust jacket. Price, $5.00. *Locations:*
DLC (16 March 1953), MAJ (10 May 1953), JM, MA, NjP, RPB, WU.

B 12.1.c
Third printing [n.d.]

Norwalk, Conn.: Easton Press, [n.d.]

Masterpieces of American Literature, Collector's Edition. Location: Lowenberg.

B 13 LOVE POEMS AND OTHERS
1952

B 13.1
First edition, only printing [1952]

[all within an ornamental frame surrounding a single-rule frame with a floral design inside each corner] [eight lines within a light green ornamental frame] Emily | Dickinson | [three dots] | LOVE | POEMS | AND | OTHERS | [three dots] | THE PETER PAUPER PRESS | MOUNT VERNON · NEW YORK

93 pp. Boxed. Price, $2.00.

Locations: DLC (23 July 1952), CtY, MA, NN, NjP, RPB.

Note: An imporation by the Mayflower and Visionary Press for 19 November 1956 is listed in the *English Catalogue* at 18s.

B 13.2.a
Second edition, first printing [1960]

LOVE POEMS | [medium bluish green stalk-and-flower-design] | Emily Dickinson | [medium bluish green stalk-and-flower design] | THE PETER PAUPER PRESS | Mount Vernon, New York

61 pp. Dust jacket. Price, $1.00.

Locations: MAJ (17 March 1960), CtY, JM, MA, NcU, NjP, RPB.

Note: Numerous subsequent undated reprintings.

B 14 POÈMES
1954

B 14.1
Only edition, only printing [1954]

EMILY DICKINSON | *Poèmes* | Avant-Propos et Traduction | de | Jean Simon | [publisher's logo] | PIERRE SEGHERS, ÉDITEUR, PARIS-14ᵉ

77 pp. Dust jacket. *Autour du Monde* 22. Published "1ᵉ trimestre 1954." English and French on facing pages.

Locations: CtY, MA, RPB.

B 15 DER ENGEL IN GRAU
1956

B 15.1
Only edition, only printing [1956]

DER | ENGEL IN GRAU | Aus dem Leben und Werk | de amerikanischen Dichterin | EMILY DICKINSON | Eingeleitet, ausgewählt und übertragen | von | Maria Mathi | [rule] | KESSLER VERLAG MANNHEIM

221 pp. Dust jacket. English and German on facing pages. Copyright 1956.

Locations: WU (28 February 1957), RPB.

B 16 POESIAS ESCOLHIDAS
1956

B 16.1
Only edition, only printing [1956]

[all within a horseshoe-shaped yellow and black leaf-and-branch frame] POESIAS ES-COLHIDAS | DE | EMILY DICKINSON | *Tradução, seleção, apresentação | e nota bibliográfica de* | OLÍVA KRÄHENBÜHL | *ilustrações de* | DARCY PENTEADO | [at bottom right in script] Edição Saraiva

222 pp. Self-wrappers. *Coleção Cântico dos Cânticos*, no. 4. Published in São Paulo, Brazil, in 1956. English and Portuguese in facing pages.

Location: RPB.

B 17 POÈMES CHOISIS
1956

B 17.1a
Only edition, first printing [1956]

COLLECTION BILINGUE DES CLASSIQUES ÉTRANGERS | [rule] | EMILY DICKINSON | POÈMES CHOISIS | Traduction, préface | et bibliographie par | P. MESSIAEN | Professeur agrégé de l'Université. | AUBIER | ÉDITIONS MONTAIGNE

211 pp. Wrappers. *Collection Bilingue des Classiques Étrangers.* Published in Paris in February 1956. English and French on facing pages.

Locations: NjP, RPB, ViU, WU.

B 17.1.b
Second printing [1967]

[Paris]: Éditions Montaigne, [1967].

The title page is the same as in the first printing. *Location:* MA (4 September 1967).

B 18 POESIE
1956

B 18.1
First edition, only printing [1956]

EMILY DICKINSON | [brown] POESIE | VERSIONE E PREFAZIONE DI | *GUIDO ER-RANTE* | [brown publisher's logo] | ARNOLDO MONDADORI EDITORE

621 pp. Wrappers. *I poeti dello "Specchio".* Published in Verona in November 1956. English and Italian on facing pages.

Locations: CtY, IEN, MA, NN, NcD, NjP, RPB, WU.

B 18.2
Second edition, only printing [1959]

EMILY DICKINSON | [brown] POESIE | NUOVA VERSIONE DAL TESTO CRITICO | E

SAGGIO INTRODUTTIVO DI | *GUIDO ERRANTE* | [brown publisher's logo] | ARNOLDO MONDADORI EDITORE

2 vols.: vol. I, cxcix, 531 pp.; vol. II, 532–1244 pp. Self-wrappers. *I poeti dello "Specchio"*. Published in Verona in July 1959. English and Italian on facing pages.

Locations: MA, NjP, RPB.

B 18.3
Third edition, only printing [1975]

[drawing of owl] | EMILY | DICKINSON | POESIE | Versione dal testo critico | e saggio introduttivo di Guido Errante | Testo inglese a fronte | GUANDA

lxxxvii, 485 pp. Published in Milan in 1975. English and Italian on facing pages.

Location: NjP.

B 19 EIGHTEEN POEMS
1957

B 19.1
Only edition, only printing (1957)

[red] EMILY DICKINSON | EIGHTEEN POEMS | [red] *"Partake as doth the bee, abstemiously"* | [bee publisher's logo] | THE APIARY PRESS | NORTHAMPTON | [red] 1957

Unpaged (14 leaves). Wrappers over stiff cardboard. Limited to 100 numbered copies, some signed by the illustrators. Engravings by Judith Gustafson, Margaretta Kuhlthau, Gillian Lewis, and Mary Alice Taylor.

Locations: MA (14 May 1958), RPB.

B 20 RIDDLE POEMS
1957

B 20.1
Only edition, only printing (1957)

RIDDLE POEMS | [red design] | *EMILY DICKINSON* | THE GEHENNA PRESS | 1957

Unpaged (17 leaves). Half leather or full leather or boards. Limited to 200 copies signed by Esther and Leonard Baskin, and numbered in either arabic or small roman numerals, depending on the binding (roman for leather, arabic for boards).

Locations: MA (3 January 1958), CtY, MAJ, MH, NN.

Note: An unnumbered copy has been noted: RPB.

B 21 EMILY DICKINSON
1957

B 21.1
Only edition, only printing [1957]

[ornate capitals] POÈTES | d'aujourd'hui | [ornate numerals] 55 | EMILY DICKINSON |

Présentation par ALAIN BOSQUET | *Choix de textes, bibliographie,* | *portraits, fac-similés.* |
[three lines printed over ornate 'P · S'] | [rule] | EDITIONS PIERRE SEGHERS | [rule]

207 pp. Wrappers. *Poètes d'aujourd'hui,* no. 55. Published February 1957. English and
French on facing pages.

Locations: MA (20 May 1957), CtY, DLC, IEN, JM, MAJ, NcU, NjP, RPB, WU.

B 22 POEMAS
1957

B 22.1
First edition, only printing [1957]

EMILY DICKINSON | POEMAS | *Selección y Versión* | *de* | M. MANENT | [publisher's
logo] | EDITORIAL JUVENTUD, S. A. | BARCELONA

166 pp. Wrappers. Dust jacket. Edited by María Manent. Published April 1957. English
and Spanish on facing pages.

Locations: NjP (14 May 1957), MA.

B 22.2.a
Second edition, first printing (1973)

EMILY DICKINSON | POEMAS | *Selección y versión* | *de* | M. MANENT | VISOR —
MADRID — 1973

138 pp. Wrappers. *Colección Visor de Poesía,* no. 39. *Not seen.* Reprinted 1979.
Location: ScU.

B 23 GEDICHTE
1959

B 23.1
Only edition, only printing [1959]

EMILY DICKINSON | Gedichte | Ausgewählt und übersetzt von | LOLA GRUENTHAL |
KARL H. HENSSEL VERLAG | BERLIN

86 pp. Dust jacket. English and German on facing pages.

Locations: MH (13 January 1960), MA, NN.

B 24 SELECTED POEMS OF EMILY DICKINSON
1959

B 24.1.a
Only edition, first printing [1959]

SELECTED POEMS OF | EMILY DICKINSON | *Edited with an Introduction* | *and Notes* |
by | JAMES REEVES | [publisher's logo] | [rule] | WILLIAM HEINEMANN LTD | MEL-
BOURNE :: LONDON :: TORONTO

lii, 113 pp. Dust jacket. *Poetry Bookshelf.* Price, 9s. 6d. The copyright page reads 'FIRST PUBLISHED 1959'. 3,000 copies printed. Published 2 March 1959. Distributed in the United States by Macmillan of New York, whose label is pasted on the front of the dust jacket. Reprinted (in cloth or wrappers) with undated title pages 1960, 1963, 1966, 1970, 1973, 1976, 1979.

Locations: BO (20 February 1959), MH (22 July 1959), MA (29 July 1959), BL (16 September 1959), CtY, JM, MAJ (Macmillan), RPB, ViU; NjP (1960); JM (1979).

B 24.1.b
Second English printing for American sale [1959]

SELECTED POEMS OF | EMILY DICKINSON | *Edited with an Introduction* | *and Notes* | *by* | JAMES REEVES | THE MACMILLAN COMPANY | NEW YORK

Dust jacket. Price, $2.00. The copyright page reads 'FIRST PUBLISHED IN THE UNITED STATES OF AMERICA | 1959'. 1,000 copies printed. *Location:* MAJ (5 November 1959). Reprinted 1960. *Locations:* NNC, NjP.

B 24.1.c
Third English printing for American sale [1966]

SELECTED POEMS OF | EMILY DICKINSON | *Editied with an Introduction* | *and Notes* | *by* | JAMES REEVES | [publisher's logo] | BARNES & NOBLE, INC. | PUBLISHERS · BOOKSELLERS · SINCE 1873

Dust jacket. Price, $2.00. Published in New York. The copyright page reads 'First published in the United States | in 1966'. *Locations:* DLC (18 April 1966), MA, MH, NNC, WU.

B 25 SELECTED POEMS AND LETTERS OF EMILY DICKINSON
1959

B 25.1.a
First edition, first printing (1959)

SELECTED POEMS AND LETTERS OF | *Emily Dickinson* | [rule] | [rule] | Together with | Thomas Wentworth Higginson's Account | of His Correspondence with the Poet | and His Visit to Her in Amherst. | Edited, with an Introduction, | by Robert N. Linscott | [rule] | [rule] | *This is my letter to the world,* | *That never wrote to me . . .* | [rule] | [rule] | DOUBLEDAY ANCHOR BOOKS | DOUBLEDAY & COMPANY, INC., GARDEN CITY, NEW YORK | 1959

ix, 343 pp. Wrappers (cover design by Leonard Baskin). *Anchor Books* A192. Price, $1.25. Copyright, 3 September 1959. The copyright page reads *'First Edition'*.

Locations: DLC (10 August 1959), CtY, MA, MAJ, NjP.

Note: Numerous subsequent undated reprintings, all lacking the copyright page reading.

B 25.2
Second edition, only printing [n.d.]

SELECTED POEMS | and LETTERS of | Emily Dickinson | * | Together with | Thomas Wentworth Higginson's Account | of His Correspondence with the Poet | and His Visit to

Her in Amherst. | Edited, with an Introduction, | by Robert N. Linscott | * | *This is my letter to the world,* | *That never wrote to me* . . . | International Collectors Library | *Garden City, New York*

ix, 326 pp. *International Collectors Library*. Price, $4.95.

Location: JM.

B 26 EMILY DICKINSON
1960

B 26.1.a
Only edition, first printing [1960]

The Laurel Poetry Series | *General Editor, Richard Wilbur* | [two lines within a single-rule frame] *Emily* | *Dickinson* | *Selected, with an* | *introduction and notes,* | *by John Malcolm Brinnin*

160 pp. Wrappers. *The Laurel Poetry Series* LB138. Published in New York by Dell Publishing Company. Price, 35¢. Copyright, 27 September 1960. The copyright page reads '*First printing: September, 1960*'. Reprinted April 1961, April 1963, April 1964, October 1964, September 1965, March 1966, March 1967, November 1967, October 1968, October 1969, January 1970, May 1971, June 1972, July 1973, October 1974, March 1976, February 1977, January 1978, June 1979, January 1981.

Locations: CtY, JM, MA, MH, NjP, RPB, WU; JM (1961); MA, MAJ (1963); JM (1965); JM (1969); WU (1974); JM (1979); White (1981).

B 27 SELECTED POEMS AND LETTERS
1961

B 27.1
Only edition, only printing [1961]

EMILY DICKINSON | *SELECTED POEMS* | *AND LETTERS* | *Scelta, introduzione e note* | *a cura di* | Elèmire Zolla | UGO MURSIA EDITORE | *EDIZIONI A.P.E.*

171 pp. Self-wrappers. *Biblioteca di Classici Stranieri, Sezione inglese e americana,* no. 9. Published in Milan in 1961. English text with Italian footnotes.

Locations: CtY, MA, NjP.

B 28 EMILY DICKINSON
1961

B 28.1.a
Only edition, first printing [1961]

[blue] EMILY DICKINSON | Introduzione e note di Sergio Perosa | Traduzioni di Dyna Mc. Arthur Rebucci | NUOVA ACCADEMIA EDITRICE

233 pp. Boxed. *Il Mosaico Dei Poeti*. Published in Milan in 1961. Italian followed by English. Reprinted in wrappers (with all black title page) in *I Cristalli* in 1964.

Locations: NjP, White; WU (1964).

B 29 TWENTY POEMS
1963

B 29.1
Only edition, only printing (1963)

Emily DICKINSON | twenty | POEMS | vingt | POÈMES | *présentation de* | Paul ZWEIG |
traduction de | Cl. BERGER et P. ZWEIG | *dessins de* | Michèle KATZ | [script] Passe-
port | 3 | édité par | M. J. MINARD | aux lettres modernes | à Paris en 1963

63 pp. Cloth or wrappers. *Passeport* 3. Published January–March 1963. English and
French on facing pages.

Locations: DLC (21 June 1963), Buckingham, MA, NjP, ViU.

B 30 14 BY EMILY DICKINSON
1964

B 30.1.a
Only edition, first printing [1964]

14 by Emily Dickinson | [five lines printed in white on gray rectangular box; the rule is in
black] WITH SELECTED CRITICISM | THOMAS M. DAVIS | [rule] | University of Missouri
| SCOTT, FORESMAN AND COMPANY | CHICAGO, ATLANTA, DALLAS, PALO ALTO,
FAIR LAWN, N.J.

[xi], 178 pp. Wrappers. Price, $1.95. Copyright, 30 January 1964. Reprinted [1964],
[1965].

Locations: DLC (12 February 1964), MA, MH, NcD, NcU, NjP, WU; RPB (1964 re-
print); JM (1965).

B 31 POEMS OF EMILY DICKINSON
1964

B 31.1.a
Only edition, first printing [1964]

POEMS OF | *Emily Dickinson* | [drawing of trees] | *SELECTED BY HELEN PLOTZ* |
Drawings by Robert Kipniss | *Thomas Y. Crowell Company* · *New York*

xvii, 158 pp. Dust jacket. *The Crowell Poets.* Also in *A Crowell Library Binding.* Price,
$2.95. Copyright, 6 March 1964. Three undated reprintings noted.

Locations: CtY (April 1964), DLC (10 April 1964), IEN, JM, MA, MAJ, MB, RPB; MA
(3d printing—November 1967), MB (*Library*); IEN, MB, NjP (4th printing).

B 32 AN AMAZING SENSE
1966

B 32.1
Only edition, only printing [1966]

[rule] | AN AMAZING SENSE | Selected Poems and Letters of | EMILY DICKINSON |

[rule] | *Selection and Introduction* | *by* | J. R. VITELLI | [drawing of elephant] | BOMBAY | POPULAR PRAKASHAN

xvi, 96 pp. Dust jacket. Price, $2.50. Published March 1966. Distributed in the United States by Lawrence Verry Incorporated, Mystic, Conn.

Locations: JM, MAJ, NcWsW, NjP, White.

Note: For further information, see William White, "Emily Dickinson's *An Amazing Sense:* Addendum to Buckingham," *Papers of the Bibliographical Society of America* 68 (1st Quarter 1974), 66–67.

B 33 A CHOICE OF EMILY DICKINSON'S VERSE
1968

B 33.1.a
Only edition, first printing [1968]

A CHOICE OF | EMILY DICKINSON'S | VERSE | selected | with an introduction by | TED HUGHES | FABER AND FABER | 24 Russell Square | London

68 pp. Dust jacket. Price, 16s. The copyright page reads *'First published in this edition in mcmlxviii'.* Published 25 March 1968.

Locations: BO (28 March 1968), BC (29 March 1968), DLC (1 April 1968), InU, JM, MAJ (1 April 1968), NcU, NjP, RPB.

B 33.1.b
Second printing [1969]

London: Faber and Faber, [1969].

The title page is the same as in the first printing. Wrappers. *Faber Paper Covered Editions.* Price, 7s. The copyright page reads 'First published in this edition 1969'. *Locations:* BO (1 May 1969), BC (7 May 1969), MAJ (16 December 1969), White. Reprinted 1970, 1974, 1977, 1979. *Location:* JM (1979).

Note one: Listed as an importation in *Books in Print* at $4.95 in cloth and $2.95 in wrappers.

Note two: An American issue of an unknown English printing has been noted, with the following typed label pasted on the title page: 'FABER & FABER INC. | SALEM, N.H.' (DLC; received 25 August 1976).

B 34 JUDGE TENDERLY OF ME
1968

B 34.1.a
Only edition, first printing [1968]

Judge Tenderly of Me | The Poems of Emily Dickinson | Selected and With an Afterword | by Winfield Townley Scott | Illustrated by Bill Greer | [publisher's logo] | [rule] | Hallmark Editions

62 pp. Dust jacket. Published in Kansas City, Mo., in 1968. Price, $2.50. Copyright, 1 August 1968.

Locations: DLC (18 September 1968), CtY, JM, MA, MAJ.

Note: Numerous subsequent undated reprintings.

B 35 A LETTER TO THE WORLD
1968

B 35.1
First edition, only printing [1968]

EMILY DICKINSON | A Letter | to the World | *Poems for young readers chosen and introduced* | *by* | Rumer Godden | DECORATED BY | Prudence Seward | [publisher's logo] | THE BODLEY HEAD | LONDON   SYDNEY | TORONTO

70 pp. Dust jacket. Price, 16s. Copyright, 7 November 1968. The copyright page reads *'This selection first published 1968'.*

Locations: DLC (30 December 1968), BO (2 January 1969), CtY, MA, MB, NjP.

B 35.2
Second edition, only printing [1969]

Emily Dickinson | A Letter | to the World | *Poems for young readers* | *chosen and introduced by* | *Rumer Godden* | DECORATED BY | Prudence Seward | THE MACMIL-LAN COMPANY

66 pp. Dust jacket. Price, $3.95. Printed in the United States. The copyright page reads 'First Printing'. *Locations:* DLC, MAJ, NN, NjP, RPB.

Note: The introduction, contents, and index to first lines have been reset; the poems are from the English setting repaginated.

B 36 TWO POEMS
1968

B 36.1.a
Only edition, first printing [1968]

[purple butterfly] | [two lines in brown] TWO POEMS | BY EMILY DICKINSON | [two purple and gold butterflies]

Unpaged (8 leaves). Wrappers. Boxed. Introduction by Philip Hofer and Eleanor M. Garvey. Illustrated by Marie Angel. Published in New York by Walker and Company in association with the Department of Printing and Graphic Arts of the Harvard College Library in 1968. Limited to 500 numbered copies signed by the illustrator. Price, $10.00. Copyright, 22 November 1968.

Locations: JM, MA, PSt, RPB, WU.

B 37.1.b
Second printing [1968]

[New York: Walker and Company, 1968].

Wrappers. Boxed. The same as the first printing, except: no colophon on p. [15]. Price, $3.00.

Locations: DLC (9 January 1969), MAJ (16 January 1969), IEN, JM, MA, MAJ, MB, NNC, NcD, NjP, RPB, ViU, WU.

B 37 EMILY DICKINSON
1969

B 37.1
Only edition, only printing [1969]

LONGMAN'S POETRY LIBRARY | Edited by Leonard Clark | EMILY | DICKINSON | [publisher's logo] | LONGMAN'S

ii, 30 pp. Wrappers. *Longman's Poetry Library.* Published in London. Price, 30d. The back wrapper recto reads 'First published 1969'.

Locations: BE (27 February 1970), RPB.

B 38 SELECTED POEMS OF EMILY DICKINSON
1969

B 38.1
Only edition, only printing [1969]

Selected Poems | of | EMILY DICKINSON | *General Editor* | AN KEATS | *A Little Paperback Classic* | PYRAMID BOOKS   [drawing of pyramid]   NEW YORK

61 pp. Wrappers. *A Little Paperback Classic,* no. 63. Price, 35¢. Copyright, 15 June 1969. The copyright page reads 'First Printing, June 1969'.

Locations: NjP, White.

B 39 GEDICHTEN
1969

B 39.1
Only edition, only printing (1969)

emily dickinson | gedichten | *vertaald door s. vestdijk* | 1969 | bert bakker nv | den haag

32 pp. Wrappers. Edited by S. Vestdijk. Published in The Hague. English and Dutch on facing pages.

Location: DLC (25 November 1969).

B 40 GEDICHTE
1970

B 40.1
Only edition, only printing [1970]

EMILY DICKINSON | Gedichte | ENGLISCH UND DEUTSCH | AUSGEWÄHLT UND ÜBERTRAGEN VON | GERTRUD LIEPE | MIT EINEM NACHWORT VON | KLAUS LUBBERS | PHILIPP RECLAM JUN. STUTTGART

222 pp. Wrappers. *Universal-Bibliothek*. English and German on facing pages.

Locations: MA, MH, White.

B 41 POEMS | POÈMES
1970

B 41.1
Only edition, only printing [1970]

[Facing title pages:] EMILY DICKINSON | POEMS | *Translated with an introduction* | *by* | Guy Jean Forgue | AUBIER-FLAMMERION [and] EMILY DICKINSON | POÈMES | *Introduction et traduction* | de | Guy Jean Forgue | professeur à la Sorbonne | AUBIER-FLAMMARION

251 pp. Cloth or wrappers. *Aubier Flammarion Bilingue 28* (copies in wrappers only). Published in Paris in January–March 1970. English and French on facing pages.

Locations: DLC (12 April 1971), CtY, NN, NjP, WU.

B 42 ESSENTIAL EMILY DICKINSON
1972

B 42.1
First edition, only printing [1972]

Essential | Emily Dickinson | (Selected Poems with Introduction and Notes) | *Edited by* | J. SRIHARI RAO, | M.A. (Literature), M.A. (Linguistics), | *Department of English,* | DURGA MAHAVIDYALAYA, RAIPUR. (M.P.) | PRAKASH BOOK DEPOT | Bara Bazar Bareilly (U.P.)

iii, iii, 180 pp. The copyright page reads 'Edition 1972'. *Locations:* AzTeS, Buckingham.

Note: For more information, see Willis J. Buckingham, "Three Studies of Emily Dickinson Published in India," *Papers of the Bibliographical Society of America* 72 (1st Quarter 1978), 97–100.

B 42.2
Second edition, only printing [1981]

ESSENTIAL | EMILY DICKINSON | (Selected Poems with Introduction and Notes) | *Edited by* | Dr. J. Srihari Rao | M.A. (Literature), M.A. (Linguistitcs), Ph.D., | *Department of English* | Durga Mahavidyalaya, Raipur (M.P.) | PRAKASH BOOK DEPOT | BARA BAZAR, BAREILLY—243 003

iii, iii, 166, 26 pp. The copyright page reads 'Second Edition 1981'. *Location:* Buckingham.

B 43 FOR LOVE OF HER
1974

B 43.1.a
Only edition, first printing [1974]

[drawing of strawberry] FOR | LOVE | OF HER | POEMS BY | EMILY DICKINSON | DRAWINGS BY | WALTER STEIN | [publisher's logo to the left of the next two lines]

Clarkson N. Potter, Inc./Publisher NEW YORK | DISTRIBUTED BY CROWN PUB-LISHERS, INC.

79 pp. Dust jacket. Price, $8.95. Copyright, 23 July 1974. The copyright page reads *'First edition'*.

Locations: DLC (2 July 1974), MA (24 July 1974), MAJ, NN, NjP, RPB, WU.

B 43.1.b
Second printing [1978]

New York: Clarkson N. Potter, [1978].

Wrappers. Price, $4.95. The title page is the same as in the first printing, except: '[drawing of butterfly] | FOR LOVE' is subtituted for '[drawing of stawberry] FOR | LOVE'; publisher's logo is to the right of the last two lines. Published September 1978. *Location:* JM.

B 44 THE MYSTERY OF BEAUTY
1976

B 44.1
Only edition, only printing [1976]

[two lines in red] *The Mystery | of Beauty* | Poems by | Emily Dickinson | By the Editors of Country Beautiful | COUNTRY BEAUTIFUL | Waukesha, Wisconsin | [four lines of verse, beginning "This is my letter to the world"]

112 pp. Introduction by Robert L. Polley. Price, $19.95. Copyright, 1 Novermber 1976.

Locations: DLC (16 November 1976), RPB.

B 45 POEMS OF LIFE
1977

B 45.1
Only edition, only printing (1977)

EMILY DICKINSON | [two lines in red] *POEMS | OF LIFE* | Anne & David Bromer · 1977

35 pp. Miniature book. Printed in Cambridge, Mass., by William and Raquel Ferguson. Published in Watertown, Mass., by Anne and David Bromer. Published October 1977. Limited to 125 numbered copies signed by the printers, 25 of which were hand-illuminated by Nancy C. Edwards; 100 copies bound in paper-covered boards, 25 copies (hand-illuminated) bound in vellum. Prices: boards, $37.50; vellum, $85.00.

Locations: RPB, White.

B 46 POESIE
1978

B 46.1
Only edition, only printing [1978]

Emily Dickinson | *poesie* | a cura di Ginevra Bompiani | [publisher's logo] | Newton Compton editori

182 pp. Wrappers. *paperbacks poeti,* no. 62. Published in Rome on 25 February 1978. English and Italian on facing pages.

Location: NjP.

B 47 I'M NOBODY! WHO ARE YOU?
1978

B 47.1.a
Only edition, first printing (1978)

[double title page of a color drawing of a rolling meadow, with printing on the right-hand side only, above a drawing of three people] *I'm Nobody!* | *Who Are You?* | *Poems of Emily Dickinson for Children* | *Illustrated by Rex Schneider* | *With an Introduction by Richard B. Sewall* | *Professor of English, Emeritus, Yale University* | [two lines within tree-and-grass frame] Stemmer | House | PUBLISHERS, INC. | [to the right of the last three lines] Owings Mills, Maryland 1978

x, 84 pp. Cloth (with dust jacket) or wrappers. Prices: cloth, $11.95; wrappers, $5.95. The copyright page reads 'First Edition'. Reprinted in wrappers in 1979.

Locations: DLC (20 June 1978), RPB, WU; JM (1979).

B 48 80 POEMAS
1979

B 48.1
Only edition, only printing [1979]

JORGE DE SENA | 80 POEMAS | DE | EMILY DICKINSON | (TRADUÇÃO E APRESENTAÇÃO) | EDIÇÃO BILINGUE | edições | 70

211 pp. Wrappers. *Obras de Jorge de Sena,* no. 7. Published in Lisbon in September 1979. English and Portuguese on facing pages.

Location: RPB.

B 49 EMILY DICKINSON
1980

B 49.1
Only edition, only printing [1980]

[two lines in script] Emily | Dickinson | [design] | [design]   Galley Press

160 pp. Copyright by Ottenheimer Publishers, Inc.

Locations: Buckingham, White.

B 50 SELECTED POEMS
1980

B 50.1
Only edition, only printing (1980)

[orange] EMILY DICKINSON | *Selected Poems* | *Illustrations by* | SUSAN GOSIN | [publisher's logo] | DIEU DONNE PRESS & PAPER | New York | 1980

Unpaged (12 leaves). Unbound sheets laid into a box. Limited to 20 numbered copies signed by the illustrator, plus five artist's proofs. Price, $400.

Location: Bromer Booksellers, Boston.

B 51 POEMS | POEMAS
1980

B 51.1
Only edition, only printing [1980]

[Facing title pages:] EMILY DICKINSON | POEMS | (Selection) | BOSCH, Casa Editorial, S.A. | Urgel, 51 bis. - Barcelona [and] EMILY DICKINSON | POEMAS | (Selección) | Introducción, chronologías, traducción en verso | y notas de | Ricardo Jordana | [two-line description of Jordana's professional affiliations] | y | María Delores Macarulla | [two-line description of Macarulla's professional affiliations] | BOSCH, Casa Editorial, S.A. | Urgel, 51 bis. - Barcelona

311 pp. Wrappers. *Erasmo, textos bilingües.* English and Spanish on facing pages.

Location: DLC (25 July 1980).

B 52 ACTS OF LIGHT
1980

B 52.1
Only edition, only printing [1980]

Two issues have been noted:

B 52.1.a$_1$
First issue [1980]

POEMS BY | [orange] EMILY DICKINSON | PAINTINGS BY | NANCY EKHOLM BURKERT | APPRECIATON BY | JANE LANGTON | NEW YORK GRAPHIC SOCIETY | BOSTON

166 pp. Boxed. The copyright page reads 'First Edition'. Limited to 750 numbered copies signed by Burkert and Langton, and 20 additional copies, marked A–T, "reserved for the exclusive use of the artist, the author, and the publisher" (p. [167]). Price, $75.00.

Location: JM.

Note: Advertised under the title *Acts of Light,* which appears on the spine and half title page, but not on the title page.

B 52.1.a$_2$
Second issue [1980]

Boston: New York Graphic Society, [1980].

Dust jacket. The same as the first issue, except: the color plate between pp. 44 and 45 and the colophon on p. [167] are not present. Price, $24.95. *Locations:* DLC (27 October 1980), MA, ScU, WU.

B 53 EMILY DICKINSON'S BOOK OF DAYS
1981

B 53.1
Only edition, only printing [1981]

[three lines in red] EMILY DICKINSON'S | [ornate capitals] BOOK of DAYS | An Engagement Calendar for 1982 | *With Illustrations by Donald L. Lynch* | [red] CAHILL & COMPANY | [drawing of fence, grass, and vines]

Unpaged (60 leaves). Wire comb-like binding. Edited by Susan Cahill. Published in Dobbs Ferry, N.Y., in September 1981. Price, $9.95.

Location: JM.

B 54 POEMS
1981

B 54.1
Only edition, only printing [1981]

[title leaf recto] [five lines in Hebrew] | [design] | [one line in Hebrew]   [title leaf verso]   EMILY DICKINSON · POEMS | bilingual edition, translated by Hadassa Shapira | ISBN 965-01-049-0 | © | [two lines in Hebrew] | Copyright by the Dvir Co., Ltd., 1981 | Printed in Israel

79 pp. English and Hebrew on facing pages.

Locations: CaOTU (10 December 1981), White.

B 55 COLLECTED POEMS OF EMILY DICKINSON
1982

B 54.1
Only edition, only printing [1982]

COLLECTED | POEMS | OF | EMILY | DICKINSON | [gothic] Original editions edited by | MABEL LOOMIS TODD AND T. W. HIGGINSON | [gothic] Introduction by | GEORGE GESNER | [drawing of tree] | AVENEL BOOKS | NEW YORK

xxx, 256 pp. Dust jacket. The copyright page has the publisher's code 'a', indicating first printing. Price, $4.98. Distributed by Crown Publishers.

Location: JM.

Note: The text is composed of photofacsimiles of the poems and introductions from *Poems, Poems: Second Series,* and *Poems: Third Series* (with the texts of A 1.1.e, A 2.1.a, A 4.1.a) rearranged in a new, more compact order.

B 56 EMILY DICKINSON'S BOOK OF DAYS
1982

B 56.1
Only edition, only printing [1982]

[three lines in blue] EMILY DICKINSON'S | [ornate capitals] BOOK OF DAYS | An Engagement Calendar for 1983 | *With Illustrations by Donald Lynch* | CAHILL & COMPANY

Unpaged (61 leaves). Wire comb-like binding. Edited by Susan Cahill. Published in Dobbs Ferry, N.Y., in December 1982. Price, $9.95.

Location: JM.

C. First Book and Pamphlet Appearances

Titles in which material by Dickinson appears for the first time in a book or pamphlet, arranged chronologically. All items are signed unless otherwise noted. The first printings only of these titles are described, but English and selected reprintings are also noted.

NO NAME SERIES.

"Is the Gentleman anonymous? Is he a Great Unknown?"
DANIEL DERONDA.

———•— —

A

MASQUE OF POETS.

INCLUDING

GUY VERNON, A NOVELETTE IN VERSE.

BOSTON:
ROBERTS BROTHERS.
1878.

Title page for C 1, first printing

C 1 A MASQUE OF POETS
1878

NO NAME SERIES. | "Is the Gentleman Anonymous? Is he a Great Unknown?" | Daniel Deronda. | [rule] | A | MASQUE OF POETS. | INCLUDING | GUY VERNON, A NOVELETTE IN VERSE. | BOSTON: | ROBERTS BROTHERS. | 1878.

Edited by George Parsons Lathrop. *No Name Series,* no. 14. 1,500 copies printed 12 November 1878.

"Success" ["Success is counted sweetest," P 67], p. 174. Unsigned.

Location: JM.

Second printing: '[all within a single-rule red frame] A | MASQUE OF POETS. | INCLUDING | GUY VERNON, A NOVELETTE IN VERSE. | BOSTON: | ROBERTS BROTHERS. | 1878.'. Listed in the publisher's costbooks as the "Red Line Edition." 500 copies printed 27 November 1878. *Location:* JM.

Third printing: The same title page as in the first printing, except '1894.' is given. *No Name Series. Location:* NjP.

C 2 THE HANDBOOK OF AMHERST
1891

THE | Handbook of Amherst, | MASSACHUSETTS. | PREPARED AND PUBLISHED | BY | FREDERICK H. HITCHCOCK. | [gothic] Seventy Illustrations. | AMHERST, MASSACHU-SETTS, | EIGHTEEN HUNDRED AND NINETY-ONE.

"The murmuring of bees has ceased" (P 1115), p. 21.
   "Besides the autumn poets sing" (P 131), p. 21.

Location: JM.

Second printing: 'THE . . . HITCHCOCK. | *REVISED EDITION.* | [gothic] Seventy . . . EIGHTEEN HUNDRED AND NINETY-FOUR.'. Cloth or wrappers imprinted 'THE GRAF-TON PRESS | 70 FIFTH AVENUE, NEW YORK'. *Locations:* MA (both).

C 3 TOTAL ECLIPSES OF THE SUN
1894

Knowledge the wing wherewith we fly to heaven | Shakespeare | *COLUMBIAN KNOWLEDGE SERIES* | *Edited by Professor Todd* | [rule] | [rule] | Number I | Total Eclipses | of the Sun | BY | MABEL LOOMIS TODD | *ILLUSTRATED* | [publisher's logo] | BOSTON | *ROBERTS BROTHERS* | M DCCC XCIV

"Eclipses suns imply" (all; P 689), p. [164].
   "Eclipses are predicted | And science bows them in" (all; P 415), p. [191].

Binding for C 1, first printing

Location: RPB.

Note: English issue of American sheets, with cancel title leaf: '*Knowledge . . . ILLUS-TRATED* | [Roberts Brothers logo] | LONDON | *SAMPSON LOW, MARSTON, AND COMPANY* | M DCCC XCIV' (Lowenberg).

C 4 A READER'S HISTORY OF AMERICAN LITERATURE
        1903

A | READER'S HISTORY | OF | AMERICAN LITERATURE | BY | THOMAS WENTWORTH HIGGINSON | AND | HENRY WALCOTT BOYNTON | [publisher's logo] | BOSTON, NEW

YORK AND CHICAGO | HOUGHTON, MIFFLIN AND COMPANY | [gothic] The Riverside Press, Cambridge

"Safe in their Alabaster Chambers" (P 216), in facsimile between pp. 130 and 131.

Location: JM.

C 5 CARLYLE'S LAUGH AND OTHER SURPRISES
1909

[rule] | [rule] | CARLYLE'S LAUGH | AND OTHER SURPRISES | [rule] | BY | THOMAS WENTWORTH HIGGINSON | [rule] | [publisher's logo] | [rule] | BOSTON AND NEW YORK | HOUGHTON MIFFLIN COMPANY | [gothic] The Riverside Press Cambridge | MDCCCCIX

Copyright page has *'Published October 1909'*.

"Emily Dickinson," pp. [247]–283. *Reprint.* See D 20.

Location: JM.

C 6 A CYCLE OF SUNSETS
1910

A CYCLE OF SUNSETS | BY | MABEL LOOMIS TODD | AUTHOR OF "CORONA AND CORONET," "TOTAL ECLIPSES | OF THE SUN," ETC. | *"Wilt thou not ope thy heart to know | What rainbows teach and sunsets show?"* | [publisher's device] | BOSTON | SMALL, MAYNARD AND COMPANY | PUBLISHERS

"Sunset that screens, reveals" (P 1609), p. 9.
 "A slash of blue, a sweep of gray" (P 204), p. 46.
 "The sun kept stooping, stooping low" (P 152), p. 130.

Location: DLC.

C 7 THE LIFE AND LETTERS OF EMILY DICKINSON
1924

THE LIFE AND LETTERS OF | EMILY DICKINSON | BY HER NIECE | MARTHA DICKINSON BIANCHI | *With Illustrations* | [publisher's logo] | BOSTON AND NEW YORK | HOUGHTON MIFFLIN COMPANY | [gothic] The Riverside Press Cambridge

Various letters and poems.

Locations: DLC (31 March 1924), JM.

American printing for English sale: 'THE . . . DICKINSON | *by her niece* | MARTHA DICKINSON BIANCHI | [publisher's logo] | JONATHAN CAPE LTD. | Eleven Gower Street London' (BL—18 September 1924, MA, White).

C 8 EMILY DICKINSON   FRIEND AND NEIGHBOR
1930

[all within ornate light green frame] EMILY | DICKINSON | · | *FRIEND | AND NEIGHBOR* | BY | MACGREGOR JENKINS | BOSTON · 1930 | LITTLE, BROWN, | AND COMPANY

Copyright page has 'Published May, 1930'.

Various letters and poems.

Location: JM.

C 9 THE LIFE AND MIND OF EMILY DICKINSON
1930

[all within an ornate double-rule frame, the inner frame being light purple] *The* LIFE *and* MIND | OF | EMILY | DICKINSON | *by* | *Genevieve Taggard* | 1930 | ALFRED · A · KNOPF | [publisher's logo] | NEW YORK   LONDON

"Because that you are going" (P 1260), pp. 123–124.

Location: DLC (21 June 1930).

C 10 GREAT AMERICAN GIRLS
1931

[all within a single-rule frame] [picture of hand with wreath] | [rule] | * GREAT * | AMERICAN | * GIRLS * | [rule] | KATE DICKINSON SWEETSER | NEW YORK | [rule] | DODD · MEAD & COMPANY | [rule] | MCMXXXI

Letter of [late January 1874] to Mrs. Joseph A. Sweetser (L 408), p. 135.
  "Death's waylaying not the sharpest" (P 1296), p. 135.

Location: CtY.

C 11 EMILY DICKINSON FACE TO FACE
1932

EMILY DICKINSON | FACE TO FACE | *Unpublished Letters* | *With Notes and Reminis-cences* | By her Niece | MARTHA DICKINSON BIANCHI | With a Foreword by | ALFRED LEETE HAMPSON | [publisher's logo] | BOSTON AND NEW YORK | HOUGHTON MIFFLIN COMPANY | [gothic] The Riverside Press Cambridge | 1932

Various letters and poems.

Locations: DLC (8 December 1932), JM.

C 12 THIS WAS A POET
1938

[all within a single-rule frame with a scallop design in each corner] [two lines in ornate lettering] THIS WAS | A POET | A CRITICAL BIOGRAPHY | OF | [script] Emily Dickinson | *By* | GEORGE FRISBIE WHICHER | [design] | *Charles Scribner's Sons · New York* | *Charles Scribner's Sons · Ltd · London* | 1938

Copyright page has 'A', indicating first edition.

Various letters and poems (P 1578 ["Blossoms will run away"], p. 144; P 1463 ["Of tribulation—those are they"], in facsimile, facing p. 228).

Locations: DLC (16 November 1938), JM.

C 13 ANCESTORS' BROCADES
1945

ANCESTORS' BROCADES | THE LITERARY DEBUT OF | [red] *EMILY DICKINSON* | [rule] | [rule] | BY | MILLICENT TODD BINGHAM | . . . *but truth like ancestors' bro-cades can stand alone* | —EMILY DICKINSON | [red floral design] | *NEW YORK AND LONDON* | HARPER & BROTHERS PUBLISHERS | [rule] | [red] 1945

Copyright page has 'FIRST EDITION | C-U', indicating March 1945 printing.

Various letters and poems.

Locations: DLC (23 March 1945), JM.

C 14 NEW WORLD WRITING
1953

New | WORLD | WRITING | THIRD MENTOR SELECTION | PUBLISHED BY [publisher's logo] | THE NEW AMERICAN LIBRARY

Wrappers. Edited by Arabel J. Porter.

Letter of [ca. 1879] to Edward Dickinson (L 605, p. 260), in Jay Leyda, "Miss Emily's Maggie," pp. 255–267.

Location: ScU.

C 15 EMILY DICKINSON   A REVELATION
1954

[two lines in red] *EMILY DICKINSON* | A REVELATION | BY | MILLICENT TODD BING-HAM | [red publisher's logo] | HARPER & BROTHERS PUBLISHERS | *NEW YORK*

Copyright page has 'FIRST EDITION | K-D', indicating October 1954 printing.

Various letters and poems.

Locations: DLC (3 November 1954), JM.

C 16 EMILY DICKINSON'S HOME
1955

Emily Dickinson's Home | *Letters of Edward Dickinson | and His Family* | WITH | DOCUMENTATION AND COMMENT | BY | MILLICENT TODD BINGHAM | *Home is a holy thing* | —EMILY DICKINSON | [publisher's logo] | *NEW YORK* | HARPER & BROTHERS PUBLISHERS

Copyright page has 'FIRST EDITION | D-E', indicating April 1955 publication.

Various letters and poems.

Locations: DLC (26 May 1955), JM.

C 17 THE LYMAN LETTERS
1965

[all within a double-rule frame] THE | LYMAN | LETTERS | New Light on | Emily Dickinson | and Her Family | RICHARD B. SEWALL | [publisher's logo] | THE UNIVERSITY OF MASSACHUSETTS PRESS | AMHERST, MASSACHUSETTS · 1965

Copyright page has '*Reprinted from* | THE MASSACHUSETTS REVIEW | *Autumn 1965*'.

Various letters and poems. *Reprint.* See D 74.

Location: JM.

C 18 THE EDITING OF EMILY DICKINSON
1967

R. W. FRANKLIN | The Editing of Emily Dickinson | A RECONSIDERATION | MADISON, MILWAUKEE, AND LONDON | THE UNIVERSITY OF WISCONSIN PRESS   1967

Various poems.

Locations: DLC (19 March 1968), JM.

C 19 THE LAST FACE
1971

[all within a single wavy-rule frame] THE | LAST FACE | [two lines in script] Emily Dickinson's | Manuscripts | BY | EDITH WYLDER | [script] Albuquerque | UNIVERSITY OF NEW MEXICO PRESS

Copyright page has '*First Edition*'.

Various poems.

Locations: DLC (13 July 1971), JM.

C 20 THE LIFE OF EMILY DICKINSON
1974

THE LIFE OF | EMILY | DICKINSON | [rule] | VOLUME ONE [TWO] | [rule] | BY | Richard B. Sewall | *Farrar, Straus and Giroux* | NEW YORK

Copyright page has '*First printing, 1974*'.

Letter of [1856?] to Edward Everett Hale (2:403).

Locations: DLC (2 January 1975), JM.

D. First-Appearance Contributions to Magazines and Newspapers

First American and English publication in magazines and newspapers of material by Dickinson through 1982, arranged chronologically. All items are signed unless otherwise noted.

D 1

"C." "Valentine Eve." *Indicator* [Amherst College] 2 (February 1850), 223–224.

Letter of [February 1850] to [George H. Gould?] (L 34).

Note: Included as part of the "Editor's Corner," pp. 220–224.

D 2

"A Valentine." *Springfield Daily Republican,* 20 February 1852, p. [2].

"A Valentine" [" 'Sic transit gloria mundi' "] (P 3). Unsigned.

D 3

"To Mrs. ——, with a Rose." *Springfield Daily Republican,* 2 August 1858, p. 2.

"Nobody knows this little rose;" (P 35). Unsigned.

Note: For further information, see Karen Dandurand, "Another Dickinson Poem Published in Her Lifetime," *American Literature* 54 (October 1982), 434–437. Prior to Dandurand's discovery, the earliest noted printing of this poem was as "A Nameless Rose" in the *Youth's Companion* 64 (24 December 1891), 672.

D 4

"The May-Wine." *Springfield Daily Republican,* 4 May 1861, p. 8.

"The May-Wine" ["I taste a liquor never brewed"] (P 214). Unsigned.

D 5

"The Sleeping." *Springfield Daily Republican,* 1 March 1862, p. 2.

"The Sleeping" ["Safe in their alabaster chambers"] (P 216). Unsigned.

Note: Dated *'Pelham Hill, June,* 1861'.

D 6

"My Sabbath." *Round Table* 1 (12 March 1864), 195.

"My Sabbath" ["Some keep the Sabbath going to church"] (P 324). Unsigned.

D 7

"Sunset." *Springfield Daily Republican,* 30 March 1864, p. 6.

"Sunset" ["Blazing in gold, and quenching in purple"] (P 228). Unsigned.

D 8

"The Snake." *Springfield Daily Republican,* 14 February 1866, p. [1].

"The Snake" ["A narrow fellow in the grass"] (P 986). Unsigned.

D 9

[Susan Dickinson]. "Miss Emily Dickinson of Amherst." *Springfield Daily Republican,* 18 May 1886, p. 4.

"Morns like these, we parted" (P 27).

D 10

"Renunciation." *Scribner's Magazine* 8 (August 1890), 240.

"Renunciation" ["There came a day at Summer's full"] (P 322).

D 11

Higginson, Thomas Wentworth. "An Open Portfolio." *Christian Union* 42 (25 September 1890), 392–393.

"By the Sea" ["Glee! the great storm is over!"] (P 619).
   "I never saw a moor" (P 1052).
   "Rouge et Noir" ["Soul, wilt thou toss again?"] (P 139).
   "Rouge Gagne!" [" 'Tis so much joy! 'Tis so much joy!' "] (P 172).
   "The Sea of Sunset" ["This is the land the sunset washes"] (P 266).
   "The Wind" ["Of all the sounds despatched abroad"] (P 321).
   "Two Kinsmen" ["I died for Beauty, but was scarce"] (P 449).
   "Requiescat" ["How many times these low feet staggered"] (P 187).
   "One dignity delays for all" (P 98).
   "Astra Castra" ["Departed to the Judgment"] (P 524).
   "Safe in their alabaster chambers" (P 216). *Reprint.* See D 5.
   "Grand go the years in the crescent above them" (P 216).
   "Too Late" ["Delayed till she had ceased to know!"] (P 58).
   "I shall know why, when time is over" (P 193).
   "This is my letter to the world" (P 441).

D 12

"Jottings." *Boston Transcript,* 13 October 1890, p. 4.

"The morns are meeker than they were" (P 12).

Note: Announced as printed from "advance sheets" of *Poems.*

D 13

"Jottings." *Boston Transcript,* 14 October 1890, p. 4.

"Suspense" ["Elysium is as far to"] (P 1180).

D 14

"Poems by the Late Emily Dickinson." *Independent* 43 (5 February 1891), [181].

"Emigravit" ["Went up a year this evening"] (P 93).
   "The Lost Jewel" ["I held a jewel in my fingers"] (P 245).
   "Fringed Gentian" ["God made a little gentian"] (P 442).

D 15

"Nobody." *Life* [New York] 17 (5 March 1891), 146.

"Nobody" ["I'm nobody! Who are you?"] (P 288).

D16

"Two Lyrics." *Independent* 43 (12 March 1891), [369].

"Called Back" ["Just lost, when I was saved!"] (P 160).
"The Martyrs" ["Through the strait pass of suffering"] (P 792).

D 17
"A Poem." *Christian Register* 70 (2 April 1891), 212.

"God is a distant, stately lover, —" (P 357).

Note: Introduced as 'For the *Christian Register*'.

D 18
"Morning." *St. Nicholas* 18 (May 1891), 491.

"Morning" ["Will there really be a morning?"] (P 101).

D 19
Schauffler, Henry Park. "Suggestions from the Poems of Emily Dickinson." *Amherst Literary Monthly* 6 (June 1891), 87–90.

"It struck me every day" (P 362), p. 89.

D 20
"The Sleeping Flowers." *St. Nicholas* 18 (June 1891), 616.

"The Sleeping Flowers" [" 'Whose are the little beds,' I asked"] (P 142).

D 21
Higginson, Thomas Wentworth. "Emily Dickinson's Letters." *Atlantic Monthly Magazine* 68 (October 1891), 444–456.

"We play at paste" (P 320).
   "The nearest dream recedes unrealized" (P 319).
   "Your riches taught me poverty" (P 299).
   "A bird came down the walk" (P 328).
   "As if I asked a common alms" (P 323).
   "The Saints' Rest" ["Of tribulation, these are they"] (P 325).
   "Best gains must have the losses' test" (P 684).
   "Not 'Revelation' 't is that waits" (P 685).
   "The Robin" ["The robin is the one"] (P 828).
   "The only news I know" (P 827).
   "The Humming-Bird" ["A route of evanescence"] (P 1463).
   "Except the smaller size" (P 1067).
   "The Blue Jay" ["No brigadier throughout the year"] (P 1561).
   "The White Heat" ["Dare you see a soul at the white heat?"] (P 365).
   "Take all away" (P 1365).
   "A death-blow is a life-blow to some" (P 816).
   "As imperceptibly as grief" (P 1540).
   Also prints the following letters: L 260, L 261, L 265, L 268, L 271, L 274, L 280, L 290, L 314, L 316, L 330, L 352, L 418, L 440, L 457, L 476, L 522, L 533, L 653, L 676.

Note: Reprinted in *Carlyle's Laugh and Other Surprises* (C 5).

D 22
S., J. H. [Julia Spear]. "Emily Dickinson." *Kappa Alpha Theta* 6 (April 1892), 117–119.

Letter of [December 1881] to Mrs. J. G. Holland (L 740), pp. 117–118.

D 23

"Vanished." *Youth's Companion,* 65 (25 August 1892), 420.

"Vanished" ["She died; this was the way she died"] (P 150).

Note: Introduced as "For the Companion'.

D 24

"Autumn." *Youth's Companion* 65 (8 September 1892), 448.

"Autumn" ["The name of it is Autumn"] (P 656).

Note: Introduced as 'For the Companion'.

D 25

"Saturday." *Youth's Companion* 65 (22 September 1892), 468.

"Saturday" ["From all the jails the boys and girls"] (P 1532).

Note: Introduced as 'For the Companion'.

D 26

"In September." *Youth's Companion* 65 (29 September 1892), 484.

"In September" ["September's Baccalaureate"] (P 1271).

Note: Introduced as 'For the Companion'.

D 27

"My Little King" and "Heart's-Ease." *Youth's Companion* 66 (18 May 1893), 256.

"My Little King" ["I met a king this afternoon"] (P 166).
    "Heart's-Ease" ["I'm the little heart's-ease!"] (P 176).

Note: Introduced as 'For the Companion'.

D 28

Howe, M. A. DeWolfe, Jr. "Literary Affairs in Boston." *Book Buyer,* n.s. 11 (October 1894), 425.

"They might not need me — yet they might" (P 1391).

D 29

"Three Poems." *Outlook* 53 (25 January 1896), [140].

"Immortality" ["This world is not conclusion"] (P 501).
    "Sufficiency" ["'Tis little I could care for pearls"] (P 466).
    "Departing" ["We learn in the retreating"] (P 1083).

D 30

"Time's Healing." *Independent* 48 (21 May 1896), [677].

"Time's Healing" ["They say that 'time assuages' "] (P 686).

D 31

"Parting." *Scribner's Magazine* 19 (June 1896), 780.

"Parting" ["My life closed twice before its close"] (P 1732).

D 32

"Verses." *Independent* 48 (2 July 1896), [885].

"Hope" ["Hope is a subtle glutton"] (P 1547).
  "Disenchantment" ["It dropped so low in my regard"] (P 747).
  "The Past" ["The Past is such a curious creature"] (P 1203).
  "Consecration" ["Proud of my broken heart, since thou dids't break it"] (P 1736).

D 33

Todd, Mabel Loomis. "A Mid-Pacific College." *Outlook* 54 (15 August 1896), 285.

"The reticent volcano keeps" (P 1748).

Note: Prior to the discovery of this printing by Willis J. Buckingham, the earliest noted printing for this poem was as "Reticence" in *Poems: Third Series*.

D 34

"Ready." *Youth's Companion* 71 (11 November 1897), 568.

"Ready" ["They might not need me —"] (P 1391).

Note: A variant printing appeared earlier in the October 1894 *Book Buyer* (D 28).

D 35

"Nature's Way." *Youth's Companion* 72 (20 January 1898), 36.

"Nature's Way" ["Were nature mortal lady"] (P 1762).

D 36

"Fame." *Independent* 50 (3 February 1898), [137].

"Fame" ["Fame is a bee"] (P 1763).

D 37

"Spring's Orchestra." *Independent* 50 (2 June 1898), [705].

"Spring's Orchestra" ["The saddest noise, the sweetest noise"] (P 1764).

D 38

Wyman, Helen Knight [Bullard]. "Emily Dickinson as Cook and Poetess." *Boston Cooking-School Magazine* 11 (June–July 1906), 13–15.

"The Robin, for the crumbs" (P 864).
  Letter of [*ca.* 1864] to Lucretia Bullard (L 1047).
  Letter of [*ca.* 1864] to Lucretia Bullard (L 1048).

D 39

Pohl, Frederick J. "The Poetry of Emily Dickinson." *Amherst Monthly* 25 (May 1910), 47–50.

Letter of [late summer 1885] to Sara Colton (Gillett) (L 1010), p. 50.

D 40

Bianchi, Martha Dickinson. "Selections from the Unpublished Letters of Emily Dickinson to Her Brother's Family." *Atlantic Monthly Magazine* 115 (January 1915), 35–42.

"Opinion is a flitting thing" (P 1455).
  "When we have ceased to crave" (P 1796).
  "It stole along so stealthily" (P 1457).

"Sometimes with the heart" (P 1680).

"An Hour is a sea" (P 825).

"The cat that in the corner sits" (P 1185).

"The butterfly in honored dust" (P 1246).

"The Saviour must have been" (P 1487).

"The Bumble-Bee's Religion" ["His little hearse-like figure"] (P 1522).

"I saw that the flake was upon it" (P 1267).

"My Maker, let me be" (P 1403).

"Unable are the dead to die" (P 809).

"Birthday of but a single pang" (P 1488).

Also prints the following letters: L 312, L 320, L 324, L 393, L 403, L 456, L 511, L 549, L 571, L 580, L 587, L 664, L 679, L 712, L 756, L 853, L 868, L 998, L 1026.

D 41

"An Emily Dickinson Letter." *Mount Holyoke Alumnae Quarterly* 9 (January 1926), 153–155.

Letter of 6 November 1847 to Abiah Root (and in facsimile facing p. 153) (L 18).

D 42

Barney, Margaret Higginson. "Fragments from Emily Dickinson." *Atlantic Monthly Magazine,* 139 (June 1972), 799–801.

" 'Go travelling with us!,' " (P 1513).

"A Dimple in the Tomb" (P 1489).

"How happy is the little Stone" (P 1510).

"Come show thy Durham Breast" (P 1542).

"Spurn the temerity—" (P 1432).

Also prints the following letters: L 593, L 601, L 641, L 653, L 675, L 728, L 767, L 894.

D 43

"Twenty New Poems by Emily Dickinson." *London Mercury* 19 (February 1929), 350–359.

"I've known Heaven like a tent" (P 243).

"The Sun went down —" (P 1079).

"When they come back" (P 1080).

"You'll find it when you come to die" (P 610).

"It was not Saint" (P 1092).

"Inconceivably solemn" (P 582).

"I took one draught of life" (P 1725).

"It was a quiet way" (P 1053).

"I tend my flowers for thee" (P 339).

"My life had stood a loaded gun" (P 754).

"Love, thou are high" (P 350).

"Why do I love thee, Sir?" (P 480).

"You taught me waiting with myself —" (P 740).

"Only a shrine" (P 918).

"I got so I could hear his name" (P 293).

"At leisure is the Soul" (P 618).

"And this of all my hopes —" (P 913).

"Saviour! I've no one else to tell" (P 217).

"Behind me dips Eternity" (P 721).

"As if the sea should part" (P 695).

D 44
"Unpublished Poems by Emily Dickinson." *Atlantic Monthly Magazine* 143 (February 1929), [180]–[186].

"I reckon, when I count at all" (P 569). ·
  "We — Bee and I — live" (P 230).
  "It always felt to me a wrong" (P 597).
  "Through the dark sod" (P 392).
  "'Twas warm at first like us" (P 519).
  "And this of all my hopes —" (P 913).
  "After great pain a formal feeling comes —" (P 341).
  "Of nearness to her sundered things" (P 607).
  "It ceased to hurt me, though" (P 584).
  "The world feels dusty" (P 715).

D 45
"Unpublished Poems by Emily Dickinson." *Atlantic Monthly Magazine* 143 (March 1929), [326]–[332].

"What would I give to see" (P 247).
  "I rose because he sank" (P 616).
  "Where Thou art — that is Home" (P 725).
  "It's easy to invent a life" (P 724).
  "Doom is the House Without the Door —" (P 475).
  "If he were living — dare I ask?" (P 734).
  "Most she touched me" (P 760).
  " 'T was the old road" (P 344).
  "The doomed regard the sunrise" (P 294).
  "A wife at daybreak I shall be" (P 461).

D 46
"New Poems." *Saturday Review of Literature* 5 (9 March 1929), 751.

"I cautious scanned my little life" (P 178).
  "Out of sight, what of that" (P 703).
  "The tint I cannot take is best" (P 627).
  "I never felt at home below" (P 413).
  "My position is defeat to-day" (P 639).
  "My period has come for prayer" (P 564).
  "Beauty is not caused" (P 516).
  "Of course I prayed" (P 376).

D 47
[Poems]. *New York Herald Tribune Books* 5 (10 March 1929), 1, 4.

"I had not minded walls" (P 398).
  "I got so I could hear his name" (P 293).
  "You see, I cannot see your lifetime" (P 253).
  "The power to be true to you" (P 464).
  "One life of so much consequence" (P 270).
  "'Till death' is narrow loving" (P 907).
  "All but Death can be" (P 749).
  "I should not dare to be so sad" (P 1197).
  "At leisure is the Soul" (P 618).

D 48
"Four Poems by Emily Dickinson." *Nation* 128 (13 March 1929), [315].

"Revolution is the pod" (P 1082).
  "There is a pain so utter" (P 599).
  "I took one draught of life" (P 1725).
  "Color, Caste, Denomination —" (P 970).

D 49
[Emily Dickinson]. *Mount Holyoke Alumnae News,* 9 November 1929. *Not seen.*

"The Robin for the Crumb" (P 864).
  Letter of [*ca.* 1864] to Lucretia Bullard (L 1048).

Note: Both were previously published in part in the June–July 1906 *Boston Cooking-School Magazine* (D 38).

D 50
"Verse of Emily Dickinson Sent to Mt. Holyoke." *Boston Evening Transcript,* 9 November 1929, pt. 4, p. 8.

"The Robin for the Crumb" (P 864).
  Letter of [*ca.* 1864] to Lucretia Bullard (L 1048).

Note: Both were previously printed in part in the June–July 1906 *Boston Cooking-School Magazine* (D 38).

D 51
"Two Unpublished Autograph Letters of Emily Dickinson." *Yale University Library Gazette* 6 (October 1931), 42–43.

"All the letters I could write" (P 334).
  Letter of [*ca.* 20 July 1862] to Eudocia C. Flynt (L 270).
  Letter of [*ca.* 1882] to Eudocia C. Flynt (L 762).

D 52
Barney, Margaret Higginson, and Frederic Ives Carpenter. "Unpublished Poems of Emily Dickinson." *New England Quarterly* 5 (April 1932), 217–220.

"To undertake is to achieve" (P 1070).
  "Dominion lasts until obtained" (P 1257).
  "The days that we can spare" (P 1184).
  "The mind lives on the heart" (P 1355).
  "'Faithful to the end' amended" (P 1357).
  "After all birds have been investigated and laid aside" (P 1395).

D 53
Birss, John Howard. "A Letter of Emily Dickinson." *Notes and Queries* 163 (17 December 1932), 441.

Letter of [October 1869] to [Perez Cowan] (L 332).

Note: Reprinted from the 25–26 February 1909 C. F. Libbie catalogue.

D 54
Whicher, George F. "Emily Dickinson's Earliest Friend." *American Literature* 6 (March 1934), 3–17, 192–193.

Letter of 13 January [1854] to Edward Everett Hale (L 153), pp. 5–6.

D 55
Phelps, William Lyon. "As I Like It." *Scribner's Magazine* 95 (April 1934), 290.

Letter of 9 November 1877 to Richard H. Mather (L 523).

D 56
"Glory." *Atlantic Monthly Magazine* 155 (June 1935), [703].

"Glory" ["My triumph lasted till the drums"] (P 1227).

D 57
"Two Unpublished Poems." *Yale Review* 25 (September 1935), [76].

"Somehow myself survived the night" (P 1194).
"More life went out, when he went" (P 422).

D 58
"If I Should Be a Queen." *Atlantic Monthly Magazine* 156 (November 1935), [560].

"If I Should Be a Queen" ["I'm saying every day"] (P 373).

D 59
"Two Poems." *Saturday Review of Literature* 13 (9 November 1935), 12.

"A tooth upon our peace" (P 459).
"She staked her feathers, gained an arc" (P 798).

D 60
"An Unpublished Poem by Emily Dickinson." *Commonweal* 23 (29 November 1935), 124.

"We grow accustomed to the dark" (P 419).

D 61
Murray, Marian. "Emily Dickinson's Handwriting Here. Mrs. A. L. Gillett Has Notes Written to Her as a Girl." *Hartford Daily Times,* 7 March 1936, p. 9.

Letter of [late summer 1885] to Sara Colton (Gillett) (L 1010). *Reprint. See D 39.*
Letter of [late summer 1885] to [Sara Colton (Gillett)] (partial facsimile) (L 1011).

D 62
Allen, Mary Adèle. "The Boltwood House. Memories of Amherst Friends and Neighbors." *Amherst Graduates' Magazine* 26 (August 1937), 297–307.

Letter of [late July 1871] to Mrs. Lucius Boltwood (L 363), p. 305.
Letter of [March 1880?] to Mrs. Lucius Boltwood (L 629), p. 305.
Letter of [1880?] to Mrs. Lucius Boltwood (L 649), p. 305.

D 63
Arnold, Helen H. " 'From the Garden We Have Not Seen': New Letters of Emily Dickinson." *New England Quarterly* 16 (September 1943), 363–375.

Prints the following letters to Henry Vaughan Emmons: L 119, L 120, L 121, L 136, L 138, L 150, A 151, L 155, L 162, L 163, L 164, L 168, L 169, L 170.

D 64
Davidson, Frank. "Some Emily Dickinson Letters." *Indiana Quarterly for Bookmen* 1 (October 1945), 113–118.

"A darting fear — a pomp — a tear" (P 87).
  Letter of [early summer 1858] to Mrs. Joseph Haven (L 191).
  Letter of [late August 1858] to Mrs. Joseph Haven (L 192).
  Letter of [13 Februry 1859] to Mrs. Joseph Haven (L 200).

D 65
Crowell, Annie L. "Emily Dickinson—an Heritage of Friendship." *Mount Holyoke Alum-nae Quarterly* 29 (February 1946), 129–130.

Letter of [*ca.* 20 April 1856] to Mary Warner (Crowell) (L 183).
  Letter of [*ca.* August 1861] to Mary (Warner) Crowell (L 236).
  Letter of [early March 1885] to Mary (Warner) Crowell (L 975). *Reprint. See Letters* (A 3), p. 427.

D 66
Weber, Carl J. "Two Notes from Emily Dickinson." *Colby Library Quarterly,* ser. 1, no. 15 (June 1946), 239–240.

Letter of [late July 1877] to Mrs. Julius H. Seelye (L 507).
  Letter of [*ca.* 1877] to Mrs. Julius H. Seelye (L 508).

D 67
Bingham, Millicent Todd. "Poems of Emily Dickinson: Hitherto Published Only in Part." *New England Quarterly* 20 (March 1947), 3–50.

"A someting in a summer's day" (P 122).
  "'Arcturus' is his other name" (P 70).
  "Further in summer than the birds" (P 1068).
  "As imperceptibly as grief" (P 1540).
  "Lay this laurel on the one" (P 1393).
  "A word dropped careless on a page" (P 1261).
  "Except the smaller size" (P 1067).
  "Summer laid her simple hat" (P 1363).
  "Heaven is what I cannot reach!" (P 239).
  "I measure every grief I meet" (P 561).
  "Is bliss, then, such abyss" (P 340).
  "Proud of my broken heart since thou didst break it" (P 1736).
  "My worthiness is all my doubt" (P 751).
  "Not with a club the heart is broken" (P 1304).
  "He touched me, so I live to know" (P 506).
  "A solemn thing it was, I said" (P 271).
  "What mystery pervades a well!" (P 1400).
  "To pity those who know her not!" (P 1400).
  "A dew sufficed itself" (P 1437).
  "The murmuring of bees has ceased" (P 1115).
  "I felt a funeral in my brain" (P 280).
  "There's something quieter than sleep" (P 45).
  "A toad can die of light!" (P 583).
  "No other can reduce" (P 982).
  "Dew is the freshet in the grass" (P 771).
  "Unobtrusive blossom" (P 1538).
  "The sea said 'Come' to the brook" (P 1210).
  "We see comparatively" (P 534).
  "To make routine a stimulus" (P 1196).

"For every bird a nest" (P 143).
"We can but follow to the sun" (P 920).
"Oh, shadow on the grass!" (P 1181).
"Why do I love *you*, Sir? Because —" (P 480).
"I tie my hat, I crease my shawl" (P 443).
"It ceased to hurt me, though so slow" (P 584).
"Hope is a strange invention" (P 1392).
"Come show thy Durham breast" (P 1542).
"Upon his saddle sprung a bird" (P 1600).
"Gratitude is not the mention" (P 989).
"Her spirit rose to such a height" (P 1486).
"Unable are the loved to die" (P 809).
"More life went out when he went" (P 422).
"The first day's night had come" (P 410).
"If he dissolve, then there is nothing more" (P 236).
"Unit, like death, for whom?" (P 408).
"A little bread, a crust, a crumb" (P 159).
"Let me not mar that perfect dream" (P 1335).
"So much of heaven has gone from earth" (P 1228).
"Ourselves we do inter with sweet derision" (P 1144).
"Too few the mornings be" (P 1186).
"The definition of beauty is" (P 988).
"Perhaps they do not go so far" (P 1399).
"The moon upon her fluent route" (P 1528).
"A little east of Jordan" (P 59).
"To see her is a picture" (P 1568).
"The last of summer is a time" (P 1353).

D 68
"Dickinson Letters." *Amherst Alumni News* 4 (July 1951), 14.

Letter of [Christmas 1883] to Kendall Emerson (L 876).
   Letter of [Christmas 1884] to Kendall Emerson (L 956).
   Letter of [Christmas 1885] to Kendall Emerson (L 1027).

D 69
"Art Exhibit at Smith College." *Daily Hampshire Gazette,* 18 December 1952, p. 19.

Letter of [*ca.* 1869] to Susan Gilbert Dickinson (L 336).
   "Her Sovreign People" (P 1139).

D 70
Johnson, Thomas H. "Emily Dickinson: Creating the Poems." *Harvard Library Bulletin* 7 (Autumn 1953), 257–270.

"One need not be a Chamber — to be Haunted" (P 670).
   "Blazing in Gold — and" (P 228).
   "A Dew sufficed itself" (P 1437).
   "March is the Month of Expectation" (P 1404).
   "Two Butterflies went out at Noon" (P 533).
   "Lay this Laurel on the One" (P 1393).
   "A Route of Evanescence" (P 1463).

Note: The first poem is reproduced in facsimile between pp. 260–261.

D 71

Dickerman, Elizabeth. "Portraits of Two Sisters: Emily and Lavinia Dickinson." *Smith Alumnae Quarterly* 45 (February 1954), 79.

"There are two Mays" (P 1618).
   Letter of [early spring 1886?] to Mrs. George S. Dickerman (L 1037).

D 72

Bingham, Millicent Todd. "Prose Fragments of Emily Dickinson." *New England Quarterly* 28 (September 1955), 291–318.

Prints the following letters: L 353, L 446, L 568, L 579, L 800, L 809, L 849, L 964, L 974, L 986, L 994.

Note: Additional prose fragments, not printed as parts of the letters indicated above, were printed in "Prose Fragments," in *Letters* (A 11), pp. 911–929.

D 73

C[oleman]., E[arle]. E. "Emily Dickinson." *Princeton University Library Chronicle* 25 (Spring 1964), 230–231.

Letter of [ca. 1877] to Mrs. James S. Cooper (L 510). *Reprint. See Letters* (A 11), p. 587.
   Letter of [ca. 1883?] to Mrs. Jonathan L. Jenkins (L 812).

D 74

Sewall, Richard B. "The Lyman Letters: New Light on Emily Dickinson and Her Family." *Massachusetts Review* 6 (Autumn 1965), 693–780.

Various letters.

Note: Reprinted as *The Lyman Letters: New Light on Emily Dickinson and Her Family* (C 17).

D 75

Higgins, David J. M. "Twenty-five Poems by Emily Dickinson: Unpublished Variant Versions." *American Literature* 38 (March 1966), 1–21.

"One sister have I in the house —" (P 14).
   "Take all I have away" (P 1640).
   "The Show is not the Show" (P 1206).
   "The Spirit lasts — but in what mode" (P 1576).
   "The sweets of pillage can be known" (P 1470).
   "The Wind began to rock the Grass" (two versions) (P 824).
   " 'And with what body do they come?' " (P 1492).
   "Because he loves her" (P 1229).
   "Bliss is the sceptre of the child" (P 1553).
   "He showed me Heights I never saw —" (P 446).
   "How spacious the wind must feel" (P 1418).
   "Speech is a prank of parliament" (P 688).
   "The Bible is an untold volume" (P 1545).
   "The day grew small, surrounded tight" (P 1140).
   "The most triumphant bird" (P 1265).
   "The things we thought that we should do —" (P 1293).
   "To the staunch dust" (P 1402).
   "What tenements of clover" (P 1338).

"They have a little odor" (P 785).
"Bloom upon the mountain stated" (P 667).
"I watched the moon around the house" (P 629).
"Morns like these — we parted" (P 27).
"The birds begun at four o'clock" (P 783).
"The road to Paradise is plain" (P 1491).
"Deep in their alabaster chambers" (P 216).

D 76

St. Armand, Barton Levi, and George Monteiro. "On Behalf of Emily: Dickinson Letters and Documents (1891–1892)." *Resources for American Literary Study* 6 (Autumn 1976), 191–198.

Letter of [December 1881] to Mrs. J. G. Holland (facsimile of a typescript of the lost manuscript) (L 740), p. 194.

Note: A variant printing appeared earlier in the April 1892 *Kappa Alpha Theta* (D 22).

D 77

M[onteiro]., G[eorge]., and B[arton]. L[evi]. S[t. Armand]. "A New Emily Dickinson Letter: A Manuscript Facsimile." *Prairie Schooner* 51 (Winter 1977–1978), front wrapper, 324.

Letter of [*ca.* 1870s] to Martha Dickinson Bianchi (facsimile on front wrapper).

D 78

Franklin, R. W. "Three Additional Dickinson Manuscrpts." *American Literature* 50 (March 1978), 109–116.

"Sunset that screens, reveals —" (P 1609).
  "He showed me Heights I never saw" (P 446).
  "One Sister have I in the house" (P 14).
  "'Lethe' in my flower" (P 1730).
  "To venerate the simple days" (P 57).

D 79

Franklin, R. W. "The Manuscripts and Transcripts of 'Further in Summer than the Birds.'" *Papers of the Bibliographical Society of America* 72 (4th Quarter 1978), 552–560.

"Further in Summer than the Birds" (P 1068).

D 80

Franklin, R. W. "The Houghton Library Dickinson Manuscript 157." *Harvard Library Bulletin* 28 (July 1980), 245–257.

"A Pit — but Heaven over it" (P 1712).
  "I tie my Hat — I crease my Shawl" (P 443).

D 81

Wolff, Cynthia Griffin. "The Reality of Emily Dickinson." *Harvard Magazine* 83 (November–December 1980), 48–53.

"Success" ["Success is counted sweetest"] (facsimile) (P 67), p. 49.

E. Material Attributed to Dickinson

Arranged chronologically.

E 1

"I Saw the Sun To-day and Laughed." *The Mahogany Tree* 1 (26 March 1892), 198.

Signed "E——y D—k——n." *Not seen.*

E 2

[Stone, Herbert S.] "Notes." *Chap-Book* 3 (15 October 1895), 446.

"A clamor in the treetops" and "If God upon the seventh day" are printed as if by Dickinson. The first poem was reprinted, as if by Dickinson, in *Smith College Monthly* 2 (November 1941), 11. Both poems were reprinted, as if by Dickinson, in William White, "Two Unlisted Emily Dickinson Poems," *Colby Library Quarterly,* series 2, no. 5 (February 1948), 69–70, and Charles Gullans and John Espey, "Emily Dickinson: Two Uncollected Poems," *American Literature* 44 (May 1972), 306–307, the latter authors being unaware of White's article, as was pointed out by White in a "Correction," *American Literature* 45 (March 1973), 117. In "Refutation of 'Fugitive' Poems reported in *American Literature;* also its correction," *Emily Dickinson Bulletin,* no. 24 (2d Half 1973), 207–209, George Monteiro points out the previous reprinting by White, and Jay Leyda offers convincing evidence that the two poems are parodies of Dickinson, possibly by Bliss Carman.

F. Compiler's Notes

F 1

Possible bilingual editions published in Japan.

I have been unable to locate for examination copies of two bilingual editions listed in Tsuyoshi Omoto, "Emily Dickinson: A Bibliography; Writings in Japan," *Jinbunkagaku-Nenpo* 3 (1973), 113–143: *Emily Dickinson: Kenkyu to Shisho (Studies and Selected Poems)*, trans. Toshikazu Niikura (Tokyo: Shinozaki Shorin, 1962), 223 pp. ("Revised edition," 1967) and *Emily Dickinson Shisho (Selected Poems of Emily Dickinson)*, trans. Kikuo Kato (Tokyo and Kyoto: Hakuyosha, 1966), 123 pp. (pp. 114–115). Professor Takao Furukawa has been kind enough to verify these items for me and has informed me of a fourth reprinting in 1969 of the Niikura translation (letter of 7 October 1982).

Appendix

Index to the Poems

Index

Appendix

Principal Works About Dickinson

Anderson, Charles. *Emily Dickinson's Poetry: Stairway of Surprise*. New York: Holt, Rinehart and Winston, 1960.

Bianchi, Martha Dickinson. *The Life and Letters of Emily Dickinson*. Boston: Houghton Mifflin, 1924.

Bingham, Millicent Todd. *Ancestors' Brocades: The Literary Discovery of Emily Dickinson*. New York: Harper, 1945.

————. *Emily Dickinson: A Revelation*. New York: Harper, 1954.

————. *Emily Dickinson's Home: Letters of Edward Dickinson and His Family with Documents and Comment*. New York: Harper, 1955.

Blake, Caesar R., and Carlton F. Wells, eds. *The Recognition of Emily Dickinson*. Ann Arbor: University of Michigan Press, 1964.

Buckingham, Willis J. *Emily Dickinson: An Annotated Bibliography*. Bloomington: Indiana University Press, 1970.

Cameron, Sharon. *Lyric Time: Dickinson and the Limits of Genre*. Baltimore: Johns Hopkins University Press, 1979.

Capps, Jack L. *Emily Dickinson's Reading*. Cambridge, Mass.: Harvard University Press, 1966.

Chase, Richard. *Emily Dickinson*. New York: William Sloane, 1951.

Clendenning, Sheila T. *Emily Dickinson: A Bibliography, 1850–1966*. Kent, Ohio: Kent State University Press, 1968.

Cody, John. *After Great Pain: The Inner Life of Emily Dickinson*. Cambridge, Mass.: Harvard University Press, 1971.

Diehl, Joanne Feit. *Dickinson and the Romantic Imagination*. Princeton, N.J.: Princeton University Press, 1981.

Duchac, Joseph. *The Poems of Emily Dickinson: An Annotated Guide to Commentary Published in English, 1890–1977*. Boston: G. K. Hall, 1979.

Ferlazzo, Paul J. *Emily Dickinson*. Boston: Twayne, 1976.

Ford, Thomas W. *Heaven Beguiles the Tired: Death in the Poetry of Emily Dickinson*. University, Ala.: University of Alabama Press, 1966.

Franklin, R. W. *The Editing of Emily Dickinson: A Reconsideration*. Madison: University of Wisconsin Press, 1967.

Gelpi, Albert J. *Emily Dickinson: The Mind of the Poet*. Cambridge, Mass.: Harvard University Press, 1965.

Griffith, Clark. *The Long Shadow: Emily Dickinson's Tragic Poetry*. Princeton, N.J.: Princeton University Press, 1964.

Higgins, David. *Portrait of Emily Dickinson: The Poet and Her Prose*. New Brunswick, N.J.: Rutgers University Press, 1967.

Jenkins, MacGregor. *Emily Dickinson: Friend and Neighbor*. Boston: Little, Brown, 1930.

Johnson, Thomas H. *Emily Dickinson: An Interpretive Biography*. Cambridge, Mass.: Harvard University Press, 1955.

Keller, Karl. *The Only Kangaroo Among the Beauty: Emily Dickinson and America*. Baltimore: Johns Hopkins University Press, 1979.

Kher, Inder Nath. *The Landscape of Absence: Emily Dickinson's Poetry*. New Haven, Conn.: Yale University Press, 1974.

Leyda, Jay. *The Years and Hours of Emily Dickinson*, 2 vols. New Haven, Conn.: Yale University Press, 1960.

Lilliedahl, Ann. *Emily Dickinson in Europe: Her Literary Reputation in Selected Countries*. Washington, D.C.: University Press of America, 1982.

Lindberg-Seyerstad, Brita. *The Voice of the Poet: Aspects of Style in the Poetry of Emily Dickinson*. Cambridge, Mass.: Harvard University Press, 1968.

Lubbers, Klaus. *Emily Dickinson: The Critical Revolution*. Ann Arbor: University of Michigan Press, 1968.

Lucas, Delores Dyer. *Emily Dickinson and Riddle*. DeKalb: Northern Illinois University Press, 1969.

Miller, Ruth. *The Poetry of Emily Dickinson*. Middletown, Conn.: Wesleyan University Press, 1968.

Mudge, Jean McClure. *Emily Dickinson and the Image of Home*. Amherst: University of Massachusetts Press, 1975.

Patterson, Rebecca. *The Riddle of Emily Dickinson*. Boston: Houghton Mifflin, 1951.

Pollitt, Josephine. *Emily Dickinson: The Human Background of Her Poetry*. New York: Harper, 1930.

Porter, David T. *The Art of Emily Dickinson's Early Poetry*. Cambridge, Mass.: Harvard University Press, 1966.

————. *Dickinson: The Modern Idiom*. Cambridge, Mass.: Harvard University Press, 1981.

Rosenbaum, S. P. *A Concordance to the Poems of Emily Dickinson*. Ithaca, N.Y.: Cornell University Press, 1964.

Sewall, Richard B. *The Life of Emily Dickinson*, 2 vols. New York: Farrar, Straus and Giroux, 1974.

————, ed. *The Lyman Letters: New Light on Emily Dickinson and Her Family*. Amherst: University of Massachusetts Press, 1965.

Sherwood, William R. *Circumference and Circumstance: Stages in the Mind and Art of Emily Dickinson*. New York: Columbia University Press, 1968.

Taggard, Genevieve. *The Life and Mind of Emily Dickinson*. New York: Alfred A. Knopf, 1930.

Walsh, John Evangelist. *The Hidden Life of Emily Dickinson*. New York: Simon and Schuster, 1971.

Ward, Theodora. *The Capsule of the Mind: Chapters in the Life of Emily Dickinson*. Cambridge, Mass.: Harvard University Press, 1961.

Weisbuch, Robert. *Emily Dickinson's Poetry*. Chicago: University of Chicago Press, 1975.

Wells, Henry W. *Introduction to Emily Dickinson*. Chicago: Hendricks House, 1947.

Whicher, George Frisbie. *This Was a Poet: A Critical Biography of Emily Dickinson*. New York: Scribner, 1938.

Wylder, Edith. *The Last Face: Emily Dickinson's Manuscripts*. Albuquerque: University of New Mexico Press, 1971.

Index to the Poems

This index of Dickinson's poems is arranged alphabetically by first lines. Capitalization and spelling of the first lines is taken from Johnson's edition of the poetry (see A 10). Each entry lists the first printing and all significant subsequent reprintings for that poem. If the poem was supplied with a title at any time, that title is given in parentheses following the printing information. Printings in books are referred to by abbreviations or short titles with dates; full titles for the former may be found in the list below, whereas full information on the latter may be found in Section C. Printings in magazines and newpapers are referred to by abbreviations or titles of the publications, both with dates; full titles for the former may be found in the list below, and full information on the latter may be found in Section D. Poems with titles are also listed in the general index to this book. The following abbreviations are used:

AB	Millicent Todd Bingham, *Ancestors' Brocades* (C 13)
AL	*American Literature*
BM	*Bolts of Melody* (A 8)
CE	The Centenary Edition of *The Poems of Emily Dickinson* (B 4)
CP	*The Complete Poems of Emily Dickinson* (B 1)
FF	Martha Dickinson Bianchi, *Emily Dickinson Face to Face* (C 11)
FP	*Further Poems* (A 6)
HLB	*Harvard Library Bulletin*
L94	*Letters,* 1894 edition (A 3.1)
L31	*Letters,* 1931 edition (A 3.2)
L58	*Letters,* 1958 edition (A 11)
LH	*Emily Dickinson's Letters to Dr. and Mrs. Josiah Gilbert Holland* (A 9)
LL	Martha Dickinson Bianchi, *The Life and Letters of Emily Dickinson* (C 7)
MSS	*The Manuscript Books of Emily Dickinson* (A 12)
NEQ	*New England Quarterly*
NYHTB	*New York Herald Tribune Books*
P1	*Poems* (A 1)
P2	*Poems: Second Series* (A 2)
P3	*Poems: Third Series* (A 4)
P55	*Poems,* 1955 edition (A 10)
PBSA	*Papers of the Bibliographical Society of America*
SH	*The Single Hound* (A 5)
SRL	*Saturday Review of Literature*
UP	*Unpublished Poems* (A 7)

A Bee his burnished Carriage (P 1339), *BM,* 70; *NEQ* (1955), 311; *P55,* 925; *L58,* 545; *MSS,* 1353–1354
A Bird came down the Walk (P 328), *Atlantic* (October 1891), 446–447; *P2,* 140–141 ("In the Garden"); *P55,* 261; *L58,* 405; *MSS,* 373–374
A bird is of all beings, *see* Of Being a Bird
A bold inspiring bird is the jay, *see* A prompt — executive Bird is the Jay
A Burdock — clawed my Gown (P 229), *BM,* 73; *P55,* 165–166; *L58,* 381; *MSS,* 1108

Index

The titles of Dickinson's poems are followed by their first lines, which may be found, along with their printing history, in the "Index to the Poems."

Pittsburgh Series in Bibliography